Is Democracy Failing?

The Big Idea

Niheer Dasandi

Is Democracy Failing?

A primer for the 21st century

Over 160 illustrations

Thames & Hudson

General Editor:
Matthew Taylor

Contents

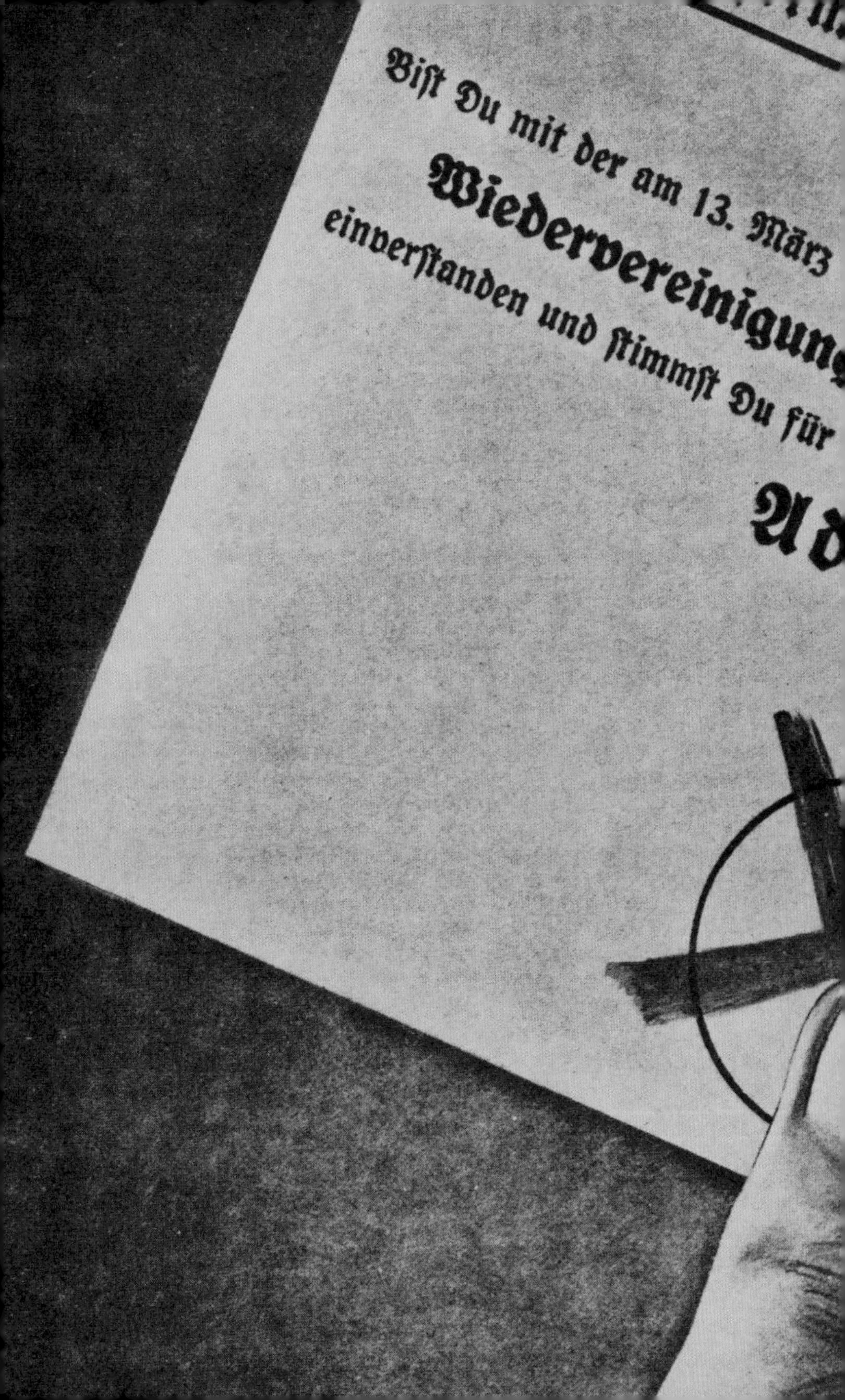

Bist Du mit der am 13. März
einverstanden und stimmst Du für

Introduction

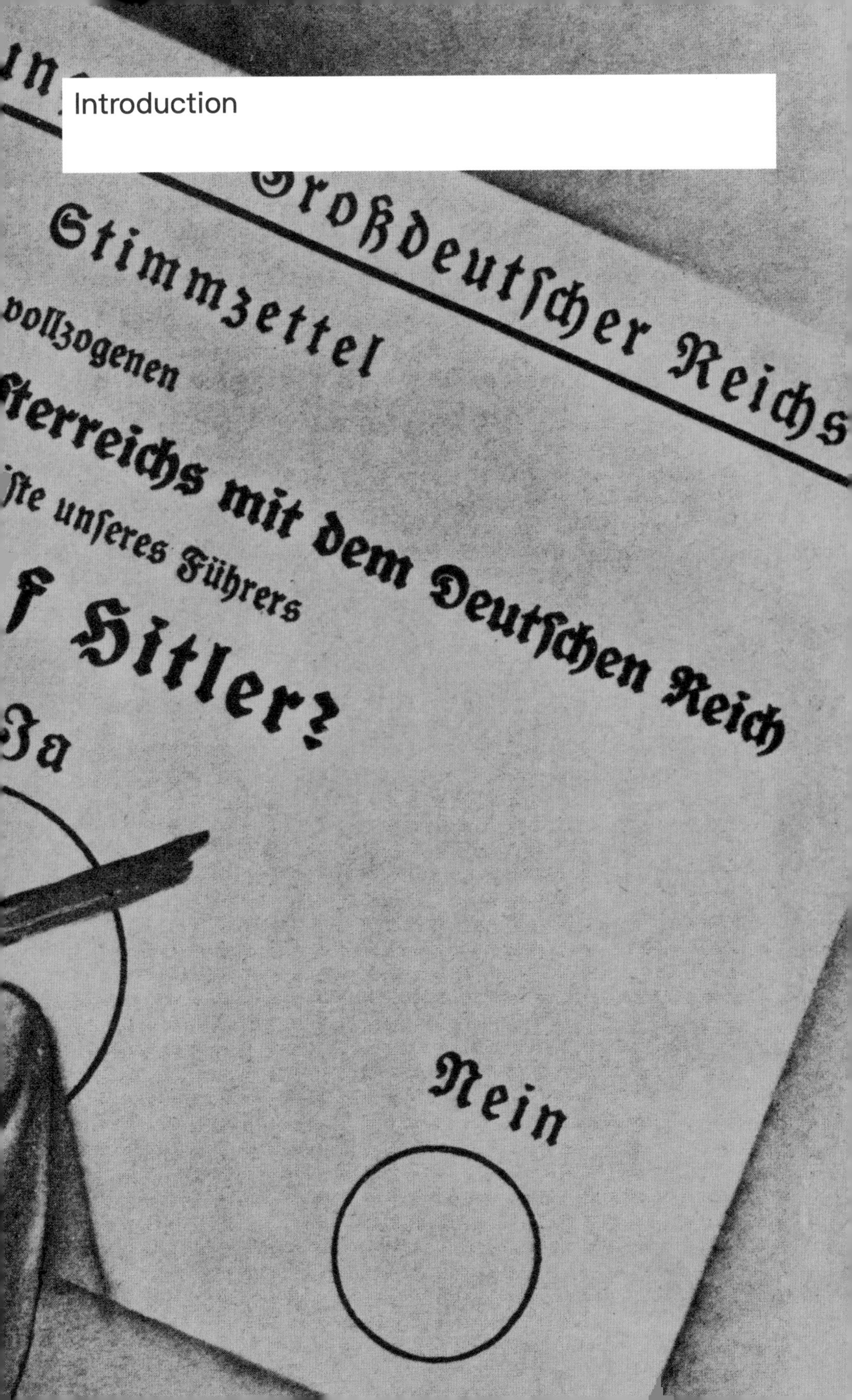

A

B

A   East Berlin border guards add barbed wire to the newly built wall in November, 1961. During the Cold War, the Berlin Wall was seen as both a physical and ideological barrier that separated the authoritarian East bloc from the democratic West.

B   The Berlin Wall, seen here in 1961, was a guarded concrete barrier that separated West Berlin and East Berlin. The fall of the Berlin Wall in 1989 was seen by many around the world as symbolizing the triumph of democracy over other forms of government.

C   The latter half of the 20th century saw growing calls for democracy around the world. In 1989 a student protest demanding democracy in China led to troops firing on protesters in Tiananmen Square, Beijing. This photograph of a protester standing in front of army tanks to prevent them advancing is one of the defining images of people standing up to authoritarian rule.

'Is democracy failing?' is one of the most important questions facing the world today.

The answer has profound implications for all of us, because no system of government in history has provided people with more freedom, prosperity, peace and stability than democracy.

Since the end of World War II, democracy has been seen globally as the political system with the most legitimacy. Indeed, the latter part of the 20th century saw mass movements around the world calling for dictatorships to be replaced by democratic governments that enable people to have a say in how their societies are governed.

But less than 30 years after the fall of the Berlin Wall in 1989 – an event that for many signalled the triumph of democratic governance over other political systems – democracy has come under threat around the world. A rise in nationalist politics has seen the advance of leaders in democratic countries, from the USA to Hungary, who have crushed political opposition, stifled free speech and dissent, attacked the press, restricted civil society organizations, curbed the independence of the judiciary and stamped on the rights of minorities. In short, they have looked to dismantle the political institutions that form the basis of democracy. Of particular concern is that these leaders have come to power as a result of widespread discontent with democratic politics. This has fuelled growing concerns that democracy is failing. However, many question this bleak view of recent trends in democracy.

Political institutions broadly refer to a set of rules, organized practices and shared understandings that govern political behaviour and interactions in a society.

The majority of the leaders who have caused unease about the state of democracy, such as US President Donald Trump (b. 1946), have come to power through democratic elections. In fact, the world has never seen so many leaders democratically elected to office. For example, in the past few years, democracy has even begun to take root in countries such as Burma, which has long been associated with brutal dictatorship. How, then, can democracy be failing?

Diverse perspectives on the state of democracy are largely due to differences in how people understand democracy. For this reason, in order to answer the question of whether democracy has failed, we first need to establish what is meant by 'democracy'.

A

B

'Democracy' is perhaps the most used and misused expression in politics. The term comes from the ancient Greek word *demokratia*, which derives from the words *demos* (the people) and *kratos* (rule of). Therefore, the literal translation is the 'rule of the people'. This emphasis on the people being sovereign – or the ultimate authority – is the basis of virtually every interpretation of democracy. But what does it mean for the people to rule, or to be the ultimate authority? This is not an easy question to answer, and many very different political systems claim to be based on the rule of the people.

Almost every dictator in the 20th century professed to have the support and authority of 'the people'. Despite being a totalitarian regime, even North Korea's government claims to be democratic; in fact, the country's official name is the Democratic People's Republic of Korea. Yet few outside its borders would consider it to be democratic in any way.

A   Aung San Suu Kyi's victory in Burma's 2015 elections signalled its transition from brutal military dictatorship to emerging democracy. She had been placed under house arrest by the military regime for years in response to her election victory in 1990, which the military refused to recognize. Since her victory, she has been criticised for failing to address the persecution of the Rohingya people.
B   North Korea is one of the world's last totalitarian dictatorships. The government, backed by its powerful military, controls almost every aspect of citizens' lives.

Totalitarian is an autocratic form of government in which power is highly centralized and requires complete subservience to the state. Totalitarian regimes control all aspects of people's lives.

This exposes one of the key problems in discussing the success or failure of democracy: it is a fundamentally contested term.

Despite being the subject of whole fields of study there is little agreement on how best to define democracy. For some people, democracy simply refers to holding an election to choose a government. Others think of democracy more broadly as good governance, or as a principle or an ideal. Others still believe it refers to a specific set of political institutions.

US political scientist Larry Diamond defined democracy as a political system comprising four basic elements: competition for power, whereby governments are chosen and replaced through free and fair elections;

A

Larry Diamond (b. 1951) is a professor of sociology and political science at Stanford University. He is one of the leading scholars in the study of democracy.

A US President Abraham Lincoln's description of 'government of the people, by the people, and for the people' at the end of the Gettysburg Address in 1863 is one of the most widely used definitions of democracy.

B This photograph was taken at Gettysburg shortly before Lincoln delivered one of the most influential speeches in US history. The Gettysburg Address proclaimed the American Civil War to be a struggle for human equality and representative democracy.

B

active participation of the people, as citizens, in politics and civic life; protection of the basic human rights of all citizens; and the rule of law, in which the laws and procedures apply equally to all citizens.

These four elements are supported by a wide range of political institutions, such as political parties, elections, constitutions, free press, independent judiciaries and many more.

We will look at each of these elements of the democratic system, as well as the different political institutions, in more detail in later chapters.

However, there are many people who disagree with Diamond's definition. Some feel that the emphasis on protecting individual rights confuses democracy with liberal democracy, which is only one type (see Chapter 1). Despite this, there are strong reasons to use Diamond's definition in this book.

First, the question of whether democracy has failed only arises if we regard democracy as being more than merely elections and governments with the support of the majority of society. Fears that democracy is failing are based on an understanding of democracy that includes the rule of law, individual rights, an independent civil society and many other institutions linked to Diamond's four elements. Second, the claim that democracy is the most effective form of government only applies to governments that have all of these political institutions. Third, there are many political systems in history that have had popular backing and even elections, which few people – including those that disagree with the definition here – would consider to be democratic.

A

A The Palace of Westminster in London is where the two Houses of Parliament meet. Parliament plays a fundamental role in British democracy in several ways, including making laws, holding the government to account, and debating key issues facing the country. The palace is a symbol of parliamentary democracy around the world.

B Umbrellas are opened as tens of thousands return to the main protest site in Hong Kong a month after police used tear gas to disperse protesters in October 2014. The Umbrella Revolution is a pro-democracy movement that arose in response to the Chinese government's decision to restrict voting in Hong Kong.

B

In looking at whether democracy has failed, this book makes several core arguments. First, a functioning democracy requires far more more than elections – it needs to ensure that all the different parts of the democratic system are working. Second, democracy is facing significant challenges, especially the use of popular support to undermine basic elements of democracy, such as the rule of law, and rising economic inequality. Addressing these problems requires a better understanding of all the parts of the democratic system and a commitment to deepen and adapt democratic processes continuously. Third, democracy has faced such challenges throughout its history.

As we will see, the advance of democracy has been complex and contested, involving many setbacks that were overcome only after immense struggle.

1. The Evolution of Democracy

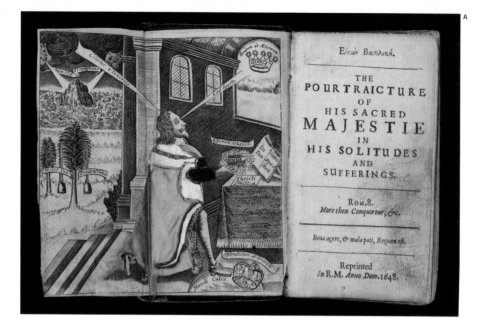

Since the earliest communities of hunter-gatherers, societies have faced the problem of how to contain and control the threat of violence. These early hunter-gatherer communities tended to be quite small, and so order could be maintained through voluntary agreement. However, as societies grew larger and more complex, achieving collective goals through voluntary collective action became far more difficult. Subsequently, societies typically dealt with the problem of violence by establishing a political order that concentrated power and control of economic resources into the hands of a small elite (as in an aristocracy) or an individual (as in a monarchy), who ruled over the rest of society with absolute authority. Those in power had an incentive to maintain peace and order so they could continue to benefit from their privileged access to economic resources.

A The frontispiece of *Eikon Basilike*, said to be written by King Charles I of England and published shortly after his execution in 1649. The book's defence of sacral monarchy was popular at the time.

B *Réception du Grand Condé à Versailles* (1878) by Jean-Léon Gérôme. King Louis XIV of France believed in the divine right of kings to rule and established absolute monarchical rule during his reign (1643–1715). As societies grew bigger, they typically concentrated power in the hands of such monarchs.

The emergence of democracy gradually transformed this political order by distributing power across society through popular participation. This was in accordance with the underlying principle of democratic systems: that the people govern, either directly or through elected representatives, according to the rule of law.

However, the spread of democracy around the world did not occur in a continuous or consistent way. There have been periods in which democracy has declined and even disappeared. The various institutions we now associate with democracy emerged at different times, often influenced by new ideas and practices that shifted people's understandings of what democracy is.

B

Aristocracy is a form of government in which power is held by a small privileged ruling class. The term comes from ancient Greece, where many city-states were governed by an aristocracy, including Athens before it adopted a democratic system. Although there are no obvious examples of countries governed by an aristocracy today, the term is sometimes used to describe systems in which a small landed elite holds significant informal power – for example, in Guatemala and Honduras.

Monarchy is a form of government based on the undivided rule of a single person who achieves their position through heredity. Most countries were monarchies until the 19th century, including England under Henry VIII and France under Louis XIV. Countries that still have monarchs today, such as Britain and Sweden, tend to be constitutional monarchies, in which the monarch is the head of state but their powers are usually restricted or symbolic. However, there are still examples of monarchs who wield considerable political power, such as those in Liechtenstein, Saudi Arabia and Swaziland.

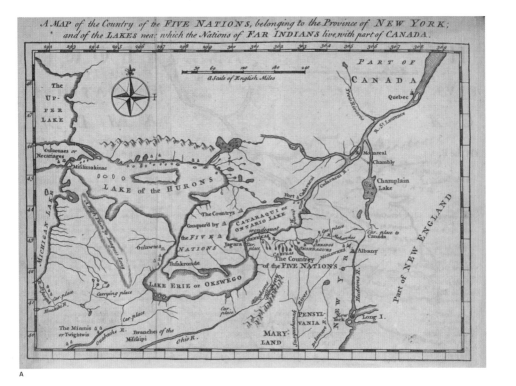

A

So where did the idea of democracy originate?

Contrary to popular belief, it did not necessarily originate in ancient Greece. There are examples throughout history of societies being governed by some of the principles we now associate with democracy. In particular, in many tribal societies around the world – past and present – decision-making has involved broad participation and deliberation by members of the community. For example, the American Indian Iroquois Confederacy had a form of participatory democracy.

Nelson Mandela has written of how his understanding of democracy came from observing tribal meetings as a boy in South Africa. During these meetings, all men in the community were treated as equal citizens who were given equal opportunity to voice their opinion in deliberations, whatever their position, and decisions were made on the basis of consensus. He saw this as 'democracy in its purest form'. However, as Mandela himself noted, women were excluded from these meetings. (The exclusion of women from democratic politics is an issue discussed later in this chapter.)

The Iroquois confederacy was an association of six Native American tribes or nations: the Mohawk, Oneida, Onondaga, Cayuga, Seneca and later the Tuscarora. These different tribes formed a confederacy in 1142.

Participatory democracy is a term that refers to the broad participation of all individuals in a society in political decisions and policies that impact their lives. There are various forms of participatory democracy, including direct democracy (see overleaf).

Nelson Mandela (1918–2013) was an anti-apartheid activist who was imprisoned by the apartheid regime for 27 years. After his release, he became South Africa's first democratically elected president and also the country's first black president. He served from 1994 to 1999.

A   This map from 1747 shows the Iroquois tribes' territory. The Iroquois practised a form of participatory democracy, in which members of the tribes would participate in decision-making processes. Many believe that the federal democracy of the USA was inspired by the Iroquois Confederacy.
B   Nelson Mandela is seen here in Johannesburg before his long imprisonment on Robben Island in 1964. Mandela was one of the most important democratic leaders of the 20th century. His victory in the South Africa elections in 1994 signalled the country's transition to democracy following apartheid.

B

A German troops raise the swastika over the Acropolis, the birthplace of democracy, in April 1941. A month later, two students tore the flag down in one of the first acts of Greek resistance to Nazi occupation.

B British Prime Minister Margaret Thatcher visits the Acropolis in 1980. The Acropolis is a universal symbol of democracy. Many of its buildings were constructed in the 5th century BC, when Athenian democracy emerged.

C *Cicero Denounces Catiline* (c. 1889) by Cesare Maccari shows Cicero, a Roman orator, statesman and writer, addressing the Senate. The Roman Republic arose around the same time as the direct democracies of ancient Greece. A crucial difference was that the Roman Republic included elected representatives.

The emergence of democracy as a full political system can be traced to the city-state of Athens, and a number of other Greek cities, around the 5th century BC. After a series of revolts that removed a dynasty of tyrants from power, the Athenians set up a system of government based on direct democracy. All Athenian citizens participated in public debates in the Assembly, and could vote on legislation and executive bills. Appointments for other public positions and duties were based on a lottery that ensured all citizens stood an equal chance of selection.

Citizenship, however, was restricted to free men; women and slaves were not permitted to participate in politics.

Direct democracy is a form of government in which citizens decide on laws and policies directly through voting or consensus. It first emerged as a political system in ancient Greece around the 5th century BC. Some aspects of direct democracy are used in the Swiss political system.

Plato (c. 428–348 BC) was a philosopher in ancient Athens. He is widely considered the most important figure in the development of philosophy. His work laid the foundations of Western philosophy and science.

Aristotle (c. 384–322) was a philosopher and scientist in ancient Athens. His work has had a significant impact on a wide range of subjects, including physics, biology, metaphysics and ethics.

Republic refers to a form of government in which power is held by the people and their elected representatives. It is also used to refer to a state that has an elected or nominated president rather than a monarch. It is frequently used to describe representative rather than direct democracy, although this distinction was only introduced during the American Revolution.

The first criticism of democracy is also found in ancient Athens, foreshadowing arguments made against democracy today. The most notable critic was Plato, who argued that democracy promoted the rule of the ignorant over the knowledgeable. He also felt that democracy led to decisions based on opinion and impulse rather than the pursuit of the common good, and that it gave rise to disorder. His student, Aristotle, took a more nuanced view, arguing that while citizen participation in politics was desirable, restrictions on democracy were needed to prevent mob rule.

Around the time democracy surfaced in Greece, popular government also appeared in Italy, in the city of Rome. The Romans referred to their political system as a republic or *res publica*, which means 'public matter'. The state was considered a public matter rather than the private property of rulers, and people did not inherit positions – as they would in a monarchy or an aristocracy – but were appointed or elected to offices of the state.

Initially, the right to govern the Roman Republic was restricted to aristocrats, although after much struggle common men (plebeians) also gained entry to government. Unlike in Athens, the Roman Republic did not adopt direct democracy. Instead, the system was based on electing representatives, and the Romans developed a sophisticated legal framework for how the people could confer their power on political leaders.

c

The suppression of democracy in ancient Athens (after it was conquered by the Macedonian army of Phillip II in 338 BC) and Rome (following political instability in the 1st century BC) led to its disappearance. There are examples of self-governments emerging in parts of India between the 6th and 4th centuries BC, and in Iran around the 4th century BC, but they were isolated and relatively short-lived. Most European countries developed monarchies with feudal systems during the Middle Ages, and it was not until the emergence of popular government in Italian city-states, such as Venice and Florence, in AD 1100 that something resembling democracy appeared again as a political system. Around the same time in Russia, the Novgorod Republic emerged, which also included aspects of democracy. However, these republics gave way to authoritarian rule after two to three hundred years.

Philip II of Macedon (*c.* 382–336 BC) was the king of the ancient Greek kingdom of Macedon from 359 BC until 336 BC when he was assassinated.

Feudalism was the dominant social system in medieval Europe (between the 9th and 15th centuries) based on land being granted in exchange for service or labour. The nobility (or lords) were provided land from the monarch in exchange for military service and taxes, vassals were tenants of nobles, and the peasantry lived on their lord's land and provided him with labour and a share of their produce in return for protection.

A   Thingvellir National Park, Iceland, is where the Althing, an open-air national assembly, continued to meet until 1798.

B   King Oscar II of Sweden opens parliament in 1905, following the dissolution of the union between Norway and Sweden.

C   Första kammaren is the upper house of Sweden's parliament. Representatives were elected from county and city councils, whose members were directly elected by the public.

A

B

C

One of the central features of modern democracy is a national parliament made up of elected representatives, with some power devolved to popularly chosen local governments. The origins of this combination of political institutions are in Northern Europe, in places such as Britain, Scandinavia, the Netherlands and Switzerland, although it took centuries for these institutions to evolve into what we would now recognize as democratic systems.

By AD 900, the Vikings in Scandinavia had developed local assemblies, known as tings, where free men could settle disputes, discuss and decide on laws, and make other major decisions. In Iceland in c. AD 930, they created a national assembly, the Althing, which is the oldest continuous national parliament in the world. In the Netherlands and Flanders, the growth of commerce, finance and manufacturing helped to create urban middle classes with significant economic resources. To draw on this wealth, rulers needed the cooperation of these middle classes, and so held meetings with representatives of the new classes from different towns.

Two fundamental parts of democracy are the rule of law and the protection of individual rights.

Therefore, an important development in the evolution of democracy was the introduction of constraints on the absolute power of monarchs. The Magna Carta (Great Charter) formally placed such limits on the power of kings in England. It was originally drafted in 1215 as a treaty to make peace between King John (1166–1216) and a group of rebel barons, by providing the barons with protection from illegal imprisonment, access to swift justice and limits to feudal payments to the king. Article 39 of the Magna Carta stated, 'No free man shall be arrested, or imprisoned, or deprived of his property, or outlawed, or exiled, or in any way destroyed...unless by legal judgement of his peers, or by the law of the land.' This provision ensured the Magna Carta placed restrictions on the arbitrary authority of the king, thereby establishing the rule of law. It also helped to introduce the protection of individual liberties, although initially this was only for the nobility.

Over time, there were other checks on the power of the monarchy. The English Civil War established the principle that the monarch could not rule without parliament's consent. This was taken further by the Glorious Revolution and the enactment of the Bill of Rights in 1689, which established the supremacy of the parliament as the ruling power and listed fundamental liberties and rights of citizens.

A   This miniature depicts the First Barons' War (1215–17). King John's refusal to abide by the Magna Carta fuelled further war with the rebel barons, supported by a French army led by Prince Louis VIII.

B   One of the four surviving copies of the Magna Carta (1215). The Magna Carta is one of the earliest documents establishing the rule of law and protection for individual rights.

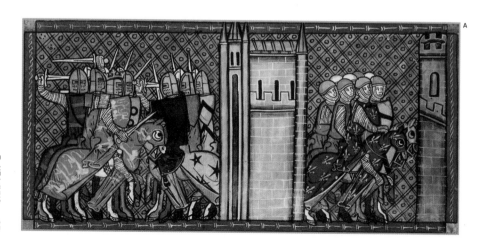
A

B

The English Civil War was a series of conflicts that took place between 1642 and 1651 between supporters of the parliament Roundheads) and those loyal to the monarchy (Cavaliers). The victory of the Parliamentarians led to the temporary replacement of the monarchy, first by the Commonwealth of England and then by the Protectorate under Oliver Cromwell.

The Glorious Revolution was the overthrow of King James II of England in 1688 by the English Parliamentarians and the Dutch stadtholder William III. It led to William III and his wife, Mary II, becoming joint monarchs of England, and to the enactment of the Bill of Rights.

Niccolò Machiavelli (1469–1527) was an Italian historian, politician, diplomat, philosopher, political theorist and writer. He was a senior official in the Florentine Republic and is perhaps best known for his treatise *The Prince*, which is a classic text on political power.

Autocracy is a form of government in which absolute power is concentrated in the hands of an individual, whose decisions are not subject to popular control or external legal constraints.

Thomas Hobbes (1588–1679) was an English philosopher. He is considered one of the founders of modern political philosophy. He is best known for his work *Leviathan*, which introduced social contract theory.

The changing face of politics from the 16th century onwards brought with it some hugely impor-tant thinkers who sought to understand the nature of the relationship between people and their rulers.

Italian statesman Machiavelli, widely considered the founder of modern political science, claimed that while ruthless autocratic rule may be needed to establish a state, or in times of emergency, power should be spread to preserve a state. He argued republics were, therefore, the best form of government. English philosopher Thomas Hobbes's *Leviathan* (1651) introduced the idea of the social contract between people and rulers, whereby individuals submitted themselves to the authority of a ruler in exchange for the guarantee of security. This meant the authority of rulers came from the people.

A *Washington as Statesman at the Constitutional Convention* (1856) by Junius Brutus Stearns. George Washington presided over the Convention in 1787, which led to the creation of the US Constitution.
B Jean-Jacques Rousseau was a Swiss-born philosopher and writer. He was an important Enlightenment thinker, who influenced modern political and educational thought.
C John Locke was an English philosopher and physician. Like Rousseau, he was an influential Enlightenment thinker, and his work inspired the US revolutionaries.

Perhaps the most important period in the development of democracy was the Enlightenment, which dominated the Western world in the 18th century. Many great Enlightenment philosophers, such as Jean-Jacques Rousseau (1712–78) and John Locke (1632–1704), presented ideas that form the basis of our understanding of democracy today, such as liberty, rights, popular sovereignty, constitutional government and separation of powers.

It was during this period that democracy was tied to liberalism. In addition, the different parts of democracy – popular participation, competition for power, rule of law and individual rights – were being brought together. Enlightenment ideals clearly had a profound impact on political thinking at the time, inspiring both the American and French Revolutions.

The American Revolution of 1765–83 saw the 13 colonies of America fight for independence from British rule. The imposition of new taxes led to protest in the American colonies on the basis of 'no taxation without representation'. Key figures, such as Thomas Paine, called for Americans to fight for independence and to establish egalitarian government.

With the support of the French, the American colonies defeated the British. Although there was some debate as to whether the new country should adopt a direct democracy, fears of mob rule and self-oppression led to the founding fathers deciding that the country should be a republic democracy (or representative democracy). Thomas Jefferson included explicit reference to democratic concepts in the Declaration of Independence (1776): for example, that 'all men are created equal' and that government derives its power from the 'consent of the governed'.

The Enlightenment was an intellectual and philosophical movement that began in the mid-17th century and continued through the 18th century, centred on the idea that reason is the basis of authority and legitimacy. It revolutionized science, philosophy, society and politics.

Liberalism is a political philosophy that centres on ideas of liberty and equality before the law. It sees enhancing the freedom of the individual as the primary problem of politics.

Thomas Paine (1737–1809) was an English-American political activist, revolutionary, philosopher and political theorist, and one of the Founding Fathers of the United States. His pamphlets had a huge influence on the American Revolution.

Thomas Jefferson (1743–1826) was one of the Founding Fathers of the United States, the principal author of the Declaration of Independence and US president (1801–09).

Constitutional democracy refers to democratic societies in which the powers of government and the rights of individuals are enshrined by a written constitution or a set of laws and customs.

Federal system is a political system whereby power is divided between a strong national (or central) government and regional governments.

These principles formed the basis of the US Constitution, which was ratified in 1789, establishing the USA as a constitutional democracy with a federal system. It also created a legislature with elected representatives, although at the time voting was restricted to white, property-owning Protestant men. Two years later, the US Bill of Rights was added to the Constitution, providing guarantees for personal freedoms and rights (including a free press), placing significant constraints on the power of government and establishing a clear separation of powers.

B

C

A

The French Revolution of 1789 to 1799 was another political watershed in the evolution of democracy. Inspired by the Enlightenment ideals and outraged by the imposition of heavily regressive taxes, the people rose up and overthrew the monarchy, establishing the French Republic. Although the Revolution did not bring democracy to France (instead it led to the authoritarian rule of Napoléon Bonaparte), it introduced democratic ideals and principles to Europe.

In 1789 the French National Constituent Assembly passed the Declaration of the Rights of Man and of the Citizen, which was fundamental in establishing the protection of human rights. The Revolution also saw the introduction of universal male suffrage in 1792 and the abolition of slavery, although both were revoked a few years later.

There was a great deal of discussion and debate on the nature of democracy around this time. Arguably, the most important thinker was the French historian Alexis de Tocqueville, whose *Democracy in America* (1835) was one of the earliest analyses of democracy. De Tocqueville distinguished between democracy as the rule of the majority and liberty as individual choice and freedom of expression. He warned of the dangers of 'the tyranny of the majority', which could violate the freedom of rights of individuals. He argued that to promote liberty in a democracy, pluralism (or the diversity of group interests) was required. De Tocqueville also emphasized the importance of a democratic culture: societies required customs, ethics, rules and norms that promote democracy.

Yet for all this theorizing, democracy still excluded many people.

Napoléon Bonaparte (1769–1821) was a French military and political leader. He rose to power during the French Revolution, and was emperor of France between 1804 and 1814. He led France to victory in a number of military campaigns and is considered one of the greatest military commanders in history.

Declaration of the Rights of Man and of the Citizen is a charter that was adopted by France's National Constituent Assembly of France in August 1789. It consists of 17 articles that state individuals' rights and assert the principles of popular sovereignty. It is considered one of the most important documents in the history of human rights.

Alexis de Tocqueville (1805–59) was a French diplomat, political scientist and historian. His work is considered among the earliest and most influential analyses of democracy. He was also actively involved in French politics during the July Monarchy (1830–48) and the Second Republic (1849–51).

A   *The Tennis Court Oath* (1790–94) by Jacques-Louis David. In a pivotal act that occurred early in the French Revolution, members of the Third Estate gathered at a tennis court in Versailles and took an oath never to separate until a written constitution was established.

B   This meeting between Pancho Villa and Emiliano Zapata took place at the Presidential Palace, Mexico City, in January 1915. The early 20th century saw revolution come to Mexico. Like the French Revolution, the Mexican Revolution (1910–20) did not bring democracy. However, it introduced a constitution to Mexico, paving the way for democracy to emerge decades later.

B

A

In most places, voting was restricted to elites. The 19th century saw huge changes in voting rights in most Western societies as a result of the Industrial Revolution and growing social unrest. For example, Britain, France, Germany, Sweden and the USA witnessed gradual increases in the proportion of people that could vote, as voting restrictions based on class, wealth, property ownership and location were slowly removed.

This is because the Industrial Revolution led to a shift in power and influence from rural areas to urban centres, resulting in a decline in the power of the landed aristocracy. A new middle class that controlled industrial sectors of business, such as factories and coal mines, emerged and demanded political representation.

The Industrial Revolution also led to a significant demographic change, with people moving to towns and cities to find work.

These workers often endured harsh conditions not only in the factories where they worked but also in the slums where they lived. The spread of political ideas among the working classes, and the realization that without them industry would grind to a halt, led to calls for more political rights. Furthermore, the threat of revolution led the elite to implement political reforms that significantly extended the franchise (voting rights).

The Industrial Revolution took place from the 18th to the 19th century, a period that saw huge transformations of societies in Europe and the USA, from being predominantly agrarian and rural to being industrial and urban. Central to the Industrial Revolution was the transition to new manufacturing processes using machines. This led to the start of unprecedented growth in average incomes and population, and impacted almost every aspect of people's lives.

A This Chartist meeting took place at Kennington Common, London, in April 1848. Chartism was a working-class movement that called for political reform, including universal male suffrage. It had huge popular support, but ended in failure. However, reforms were gradually introduced in the following decades.

B The Industrial Revolution saw workers, such as those seen here at Smith's Woolcombing Works, Bradford, England, move to cities to work in factories, often facing harsh conditions. They grew more politicized and more aware that industry was dependent on them, which meant they could demand more political rights.

B

A

It is a common assumption that by the beginning of the 20th century, democracy was well established in the USA and much of Western Europe. However, in 1914 only 30% of adults over the age of 20 were allowed to vote in Britain.

This falls well below any minimum threshold that we would accept as democratic by today's standards. Only men of a certain income could vote in Britain. Women did not have the vote in most countries in the world at the beginning of the 20th century. In fact, women were not allowed to vote in any of the 'democracies' discussed so far.

Emmeline Pankhurst (1858–1928) was a political activist and the leader of the British suffragette movement. She played a crucial role in winning the right to vote in Britain and is widely considered one of the most important figures of the 20th century.

Anarchism is a political ideology that believes in the abolition of all government, and organizing society on the basis of voluntary and cooperative relations, without the use of force. It is based on a belief in political and economic equality.

Campaigns to extend the franchise to women emerged in the late 19th and early 20th centuries as part of broader women's rights movements. The first country to grant women voting rights was New Zealand in 1893. Finland was the first European country to extend the franchise to women in 1907. In Britain, the suffragettes, led by Emmeline Pankhurst, adopted an increasingly radical approach in their struggle for women's voting rights, which included chaining themselves to railings, damaging property and arson. Between 1900 and 1914, around 1,000 suffragettes were imprisoned in Britain. It was only after World War I that women were allowed to vote in Britain (1918) and the USA (1920). In Switzerland, women could not vote in federal elections until 1971.

The late 19th and early 20th centuries saw the rise of political ideologies that challenged liberal democracy, such as anarchism, communism and fascism. All three rejected representative democracy.

Communism is a political ideology that believes in the establishment of a society based on the common ownership of the means of production, and the absence of social classes, money and the state. It sees class struggle as the means towards achieving this end.

Fascism is a political ideology that advocates dictatorial leadership, a singular collective identity and the total mass mobilization of society to deal with external threats. It demands dictatorial power, forcible suppression of opposition and control of the economy.

A   Suffragettes march in London in c. 1912. The long political struggle by the suffragettes eventually led to women being given the right to vote in Britain after World War I.
B   Seen here at Parliament House, India, in 1976, Sirimavo Bandaranaike (left) was the first women to be elected head of government anywhere in the world when she became Prime Minister of Ceylon (now Sri Lanka) in 1960. Six years later, Indira Gandhi (right) became the second, when she became Prime Minister of India.

A

According to communism and anarchism, liberal democracy represents the interests of the ruling capitalist class.

For communists, such as Karl Marx, government always entails one social class dominating the others, and so Marx believed that the working classes should rule over the other classes (the dictatorship of the proletariat) until a classless society could be achieved. Anarchists view government itself as the principal source of oppression, regardless of whether it is democratic or not. By contrast, the rejection of democracy by fascists is based on a belief in the need for the complete mobilization of society under a totalitarian one-party state to protect the nation from threats.

Karl Marx (1818–83) was a Prussian-born philosopher, economist, political theorist and revolutionary socialist. His work focused on how human societies develop through class struggle. His ideas, which are collectively referred to as Marxism, have had a huge influence on communism and socialism. He is universally considered one of the most influential figures in human history.

The early 20th century saw the emergence of several communist and fascist governments in Europe. In Russia, the revolution of 1917 ended the absolute rule of the tsar and brought a communist government led by Vladimir Lenin to power. The Wall Street Crash of 1929 and its devastating economic impact triggered the rise of fascism in Europe and South America. Led by Adolf Hitler the Nazi Party took power in Germany in 1933, which in turn strengthened the fascist regime of Benito Mussolini in Italy.

Vladimir Lenin (1870–1924) was the leader of Russia and later the Soviet Union from 1918 to 1924. He was also a communist revolutionary, politician and political theorist. Lenin led the Bolshevik revolution in Russia, creating a one-party communist state.

Adolf Hitler (1889–1945) was a German politician, who was the leader of the Nazi Party and of Nazi Germany between 1934 and 1945. He is the most notorious dictator in world history. His dictatorial rule was brutally repressive and he was responsible for the Holocaust. His decision to invade Poland triggered World War II.

Benito Mussolini (1883–1945) was an Italian politician. He was the leader of the National Fascist Party and the leader of Italy between 1922 and 1943. He became prime minister in 1922 and in 1925, and turned Italy into a fascist dictatorship.

A   Lenin is pictured addressing troops in Red Square in May 1919. He opposed representative democracy, describing it as a system in which 'the oppressed are allowed once every few years to decide which particular representatives of the oppressing class shall represent and repress them in parliament'.
B   Hitler, Mussolini and Italian Marshal Rodolfo Graziani visit the Eastern Front headquarters in August 1941, during the invasion of the Soviet Union.

B

The Spanish Civil War (1936–39) was widely viewed as a conflict between democracy and fascism. Together with the communists and anarchists, the democratic Spanish Republic fought the nationalists led by General Franco. The defeat of the republicans by the nationalists (aided by Hitler's and Mussolini's forces) led to a dictatorship in Spain that lasted until 1975.

During World War II, the battle between fascism and democracy was elevated to a global scale. However, the Allies' defeat of Nazi Germany, fascist Italy and imperial Japan brought about the demise of fascism as a prominent form of government.

A

A   This British National Council of Labour poster encouraging support for the fight for democracy during the Spanish Civil War shows General Franco with a swastika.
B   Male and female militia fighters march at the beginning of the Spanish Civil War in July 1936. The war is viewed as a conflict between democracy and fascism.
C   Supported by German and Italian war planes, Franco's nationalist forces attacked civilians in places such as Guernica. This anti-fascist poster encourages assistance for Spanish people during the Spanish Civil War.
D   This Falange (or nationalist) poster from the Spanish Civil War urges people to 'Take arms and fight for the Fatherland'. Franco's forces defeated the democratic Spanish Republic, communists and anarchists in 1939.
E   This Spanish Civil War poster, presenting nationalist propaganda, features the slogan 'Spain you are now free'. The nationalist victory led to a dictatorship in Spain that lasted until 1975.

B

As German-born political theorist Hannah Arendt (1906–75) explained in her book *The Origins of Totalitarianism* (1951), both communism and fascism differ substantially from the tyrannies of past centuries. They are totalitarian systems, in that they seek to control all aspects of social life. Like democracy, they are based on popular support. They derive their mass appeal from their ideologies, which provide simple answers to complex and difficult questions about the world.

The principal difference between democracy and the totalitarian systems of communism and fascism is the emphasis placed by democracies on choice, pluralism, limits on government and individual rights.

C

D

E

A

An important development in the aftermath of World War II was the signing of the Universal Declaration of Human Rights (UDHR) in 1948. The UDHR did not focus explicitly on democracy, but instead sought to promote human rights more broadly after the horrors of the Holocaust. It did, however, establish democracy as the political system most supportive of human rights protection.

Democratic principles are enshrined within the UDHR. This is most evident in Article 21(3), which states, 'The will of the people shall be the basis of the authority of government; this shall be expressed in periodic and genuine elections which shall be by universal and equal suffrage and shall be held by secret vote or by equivalent free voting procedures.' The UDHR is not legally binding, yet it is perhaps the most influential international declaration that has ever been signed. It is used frequently to promote democratic rights, and to pressure governments that violate these rights.

The end of World War II also put in motion the process of decolonization, which led to the globalization of democracy, spreading democracy to regions of the world that had for decades or even centuries been subject to repressive and authoritarian rule by foreign powers. Countries across Africa, Asia and the Caribbean gained independence from European colonial rule following national liberation movements rooted in the democratic ideals of people's right to self-determination.

National liberation movements were inspired and led by figures such as Mahatma Gandhi, Kwame Nkrumah and Frantz Fanon. Many of these individuals had studied in Europe and had witnessed first-hand the hypocrisy and inherent racism of a colonial system based on democratic European countries subjecting those living in the colonies to dictatorial rule.

Mohandas 'Mahatma' Gandhi (1869–1948) was a lawyer, philosopher and the leader of the Indian independence movement, which secured India's independence from Britain through a mass-based non-violent movement. He is considered the 'Father of the Nation'.

Kwame Nkrumah (1909–72) was the first prime minister and president of Ghana. He led Ghana to independence in 1957, having previously founded the Convention People's Party. He was a big advocate of Pan-Africanism and was a founding member of the Organisation of African Unity.

Frantz Fanon (1925–61) was a Martinique-born psychiatrist, philosopher, revolutionary and writer. His work focused on colonialism and the consequences of decolonization, inspiring many national liberation movements.

A   Seen here with diplomat P. C. Jessup at the United Nations conference in Paris in 1948, Eleanor Roosevelt, the First Lady of the USA, was one of the chief architects of the UDHR. It is arguably the most important international agreement in existence, guaranteeing the fundamental human rights of people around the world.

B   The Duchess of Kent is pictured at the Ghana independence ceremony in 1957. Ghana was the first Sub-Saharan African country to gain independence, triggering the process of decolonization across Africa.

B

A

The independence movement in India, led by Gandhi, Jawaharlal Nehru and other key figures, was a mass-based campaign that used tactics of non-violent resistance and civil disobedience. The movement had its roots in a soldiers' rebellion against British rule in 1857.

After Gandhi's return from South Africa in 1915, it became a movement based on popular support and non-violent resistance. Key events in the independence struggle included the massacre of unarmed protesters in Amritsar in 1919 by British troops, the Salt March led by Gandhi in 1930 to protest the Salt Tax (which effectively made it illegal to sell or produce salt) and the boycott of British goods in 1937. On gaining independence in August 1947, India adopted a parliamentary system with universal suffrage, thereby becoming the world's largest democracy.

B

Although decolonization occurred en masse after World War II, there are notable examples of colonies seeking self-determination before this, as in the case of the USA. One of the most important liberation struggles took place in Haiti. The Haitian Revolution (1791–1804), led by Toussaint L'Ouverture, saw slaves in the colony overthrow their masters and then defeat a French force sent by Napoléon to crush the revolution. Haiti became the first black republic, and at the time it was only the second republic in the Western hemisphere.

A This Quit India demonstration took place in Bombay in August 1942. The movement succeeded in securing the country's independence from British rule five years later, whereupon India became the world's largest democracy. It was based on mass participation and inspired civil society movements around the globe.

B Mahatma Gandhi's secretary is seen here addressing a huge crowd in Bombay in May 1930. A motion was passed to boycott British goods following the civil disobedience riots and demonstrations, and the arrest of Gandhi. The boycott was a key tactic.

C This painting (c. 187) by George DeBaptiste depicts former slave Toussant L'Ouverture. He was the leader of the Haitian Revolution, the only slave revolt that led to the founding of a nation.

C

Jawaharlal Nehru (1889–1964) was the first prime minister of India and one of the leaders of India's independence movement. He was prime minister between 1947 and 1964 and is widely considered to be the architect of the modern Indian state.

Toussaint L'Ouverture (1743–1803) was the leader of the Haitian Revolution, which saw the end of slavery and the independence of Haiti. His military and political expertise are seen as crucial in the establishment of Haiti as a republic.

A

Colonialism was not the only way in which racism undermined individual rights in democracies.

In the first half of the 20th century, ethnic minorities were denied basic civil and political rights in many democratic countries. In the USA, it was not until the Voting Rights Act was passed in 1965 – at the height of the Civil Rights Movement – that Native Americans and African Americans had full voting rights across the country.

Similarly, it was in 1965 that indigenous Australians were granted full voting rights across Australia. However, discriminatory policies continued in many democracies long after this. It is not only ethnic minorities that have faced such prejudice; for most of the 20th century sexual minorities in the majority of democratic countries have faced discriminatory policies. This includes homosexuality being illegal in parts of Britain until 1982 and in parts of the USA until 2003.

B

The Civil Rights Movement broadly refers to social movements in the USA during the 1950s and 1960s that sought to bring an end to racial segregation and discrimination against African Americans, and to ensure their civil and political rights were protected. The movement worked with Congress to introduce important legislation that overturned discriminatory practices.

The end of colonialism, together with the civil rights and then gay rights movements, helped to establish the principle that everyone is entitled to basic civil and political rights regardless of their gender, race, religion or sexual preference.

A   This photograph depicts an example of racial segregation in North Carolina in 1950. The Jim Crow laws introduced in the USA in the late 19th century segregated African Americans and Whites. Signs like this were used to show non-white Americans where they were legally allowed to drink, eat, walk and rest. African Americans and other non-white Americans were also denied full voting rights. Such racial discrimination is a severe violation of people's basic rights and undermines the functioning of democracy.

B   Civil Rights leader Martin Luther King waves to supporters during the 'March on Washington' in August 1963. King said the march was 'the greatest demonstration of freedom in the history of the United States'. The Civil Rights Movement in the USA demanded equal rights for citizens regardless of the colour of their skin. It succeeded in ending racial segregation in the late 1960s.

A

B

Francis Fukuyama (b. 1952) is a US political scientist and author. He has written extensively on the subject of political order and is best known for his book *The End of History and the Last Man* (1992).

The fall of the Berlin Wall in 1989 signalled the end of the Cold War, which had pitched the liberal democracy of the West against the authoritarian communism of the Soviet-led Eastern bloc. Yet, as explored in Chapter 3, both sides were willing to undermine democracy in the developing world in order to further their own political and economic interests.

The demise of the Soviet Union led to a dramatic global change.

US political scientist Francis Fukuyama argued that it signified the 'end of history', in that it represented the triumph of liberal democracy over other ideologies and forms of government and led to a wave of democratization across Eastern Europe.

Social movements in countries such as East Germany, Poland and Czechoslovakia were fundamental in driving this shift towards democracy.

In Latin America, too, the military regimes gave way to democratically elected governments, following broad movements for democracy.

A   Polish Solidarity leader Lech Walesa is seen here addressing striking workers at the Lenin Shipyard in Gdańsk in 1988. Solidarity was founded at the shipyard in 1980 as an independent trade union. It evolved into a broad social movement that helped end communist rule.

B   Walesa addresses Warsaw University students in 1989. Solidarity used civil resistance to promote social change. The government responded with repression. However, semi-free elections were held in 1989, and a Solidarity-led coalition formed a government with Walesa elected president.

C   Evo Morales became president of Bolivia in 2006, on the back of a social movement in the country that was transformed into the political party Movement for Socialism (MAS). He was the country's first president to come from an indigenous background.

C

A

US political scientist Samuel Huntington labelled this the 'Third Wave' of democratization. Beginning with the democratization of Spain and Portugal in the mid 1970s, democracy spread to Latin America, Eastern Europe and many African countries. A number of factors explain this shift, such as the decreasing legitimacy of authoritarian regimes due to poor economic performance, and the increasing global recognition of the importance of democratic processes.

A   This snaking queue comprises people waiting outside the polling station in the black township of Soweto during the 1994 South African elections. The majority of the country's 22 million citizens were voting for the first time, as it was the first election in which people of all races could take part.

B   These photographs depict the passion of the protesters in Tahir Square, Egypt. In 2010 the Arab Spring erupted across the Middle East with calls for democracy. Although the protests led to the removal of repressive dictators from power, this consequence resulted in new autocratic regimes emerging and large-scale violent conflict, rather than democratization.

Samuel Huntington (1927–2008) was a US political scientist and adviser. His work focused on political development, international relations and comparative government. He spent most of his career at Harvard University and is perhaps best known for his book *The Clash of Civilizations and the Remaking of the World Order* (1996).

This spread of democracy continued through the 1990s with the end of apartheid in South Africa and the election of Nelson Mandela as president.

By the start of the 21st century, democracy had reached every region of the world. There have also been mass movements calling for democracy in autocratic countries, such as China and in the Middle East, although these have often been violently suppressed by those intent on keeping power in the hands of the few.

B

2. How Democracy Works

A

B

The principle at the heart of democratic government is that the people are sovereign.

In other words, the people are the highest authority, and elected representatives are accountable to the people. This is the biggest difference between democracies and other forms of government.

Beyond this, however, there are significant variations in the types of democratic system in operation around the world. Therefore, crucial questions are: what features do democracies share? And how do different parts of the democratic system improve the lives of citizens?

C

D

A Voter turnout badge. Voting is a key right and responsibility for citizens in democracies.

B Pro-European Union badge. In democracies people can freely express their political views.

C Obama 2008 campaign badge. Political campaigning is a fundamental feature of democracies.

D Green Party badge. In democracies people should be able to choose between different political perspectives.

To answer these questions, we return to Larry Diamond's four key elements of democracy described in the introduction. These elements are supported by a wide range of political institutions. Although the specific political institutions may vary considerably in different contexts, the four basic elements are present in all democracies.

The first fundamental element of a democratic system is that there must be genuine competition of power. The main way to ensure there is competition of power is by holding free and fair elections, in which people can elect their governments and other representatives.

Elections are a crucial part of democracy.

紧跟伟大领袖毛主席奋勇前进!

A

ВЫБЕРЕМ ДОСТОЙНЫХ!

B

In a democratic country, enfranchised citizens have the ability to vote the current government out of office if they feel that the policies it has implemented have been unsatisfactory, or if they think there is a better alternative on offer. Citizens of autocratic countries do not have this option. So, even though the Chinese leader Mao Zedong's efforts to transform the country during the Great Leap Forward were a disaster, the Chinese public could not vote him out of power.

While elections are central to all democracies, the specific rules and processes of elections vary from one country to the next.

This can have significant implications for how the country is governed. There are, for example, variations in how heads of government are elected in different democratic systems. In countries that have a presidential system, such as the USA, citizens vote directly

Mao Zedong (1893–1976) was a Chinese communist revolutionary, the founding father of the People's Republic of China, and chairman of the Communist Party from its establishment in 1949 until his death in 1976.

The Great Leap Forward was an economic and social initiative in China introduced by the Communist Party between 1958 and 1962. Its objective was to transform China rapidly from an agrarian economy to an industrialized socialist country through industrialization and collectivization. It brought about famine, causing tens of millions to die.

Presidential system is a form of democracy based on republicanism, in which the head of government leads the executive branch (responsible for executing and enforcing the law), which is separate from the legislative branch (responsible for making laws). This system is used in much of the USA, and in South America and Africa.

A Chinese Communist Party poster, 1969. Unelected leaders such as Chairman Mao had little public accountability.
B Voting poster from the Soviet Union. Elections are held in authoritarian countries, but citizens generally have no meaningful choice.
C Poster featuring Cuban leader Fidel Castro and Soviet Leader Nikita Khrushchev, two prominent authoritarian leaders during the Cold War.
D Campaign poster for John F. Kennedy, who became US president in 1961, after defeating Richard Nixon in the 1960 election.

for the head of the government (president). However, in countries with a parliamentary system, such as Britain, citizens usually vote for the person who will represent their local area (constituency) in the legislature. The political party that wins the most seats then forms the government and decides the head of that government (prime minister).

There can also be differences in how the vote share determines the make-up of the national government.

Parliamentary system is a form of democracy in which the executive branch has direct or indirect support from the legislative branch. This means the parliament makes and executes laws. The head of government (prime minister) is typically different from the head of state. It is used in countries such as Australia, Canada, India and Britain.

Proportional representation is an electoral system in which the elected body proportionally reflects the preferences of the electorate. In other words, the share of the overall votes that a political party receives translates into the share of seats it receives so that all votes contribute to the make-up of government. It is used in South America and Europe.

Some countries have a voting system based on proportional representation, in which people vote for different parties, and the proportion of votes a political party receives translates into representation in government. Other countries employ a first-past-the-post voting system, in which people vote for individual candidates in their constituency, and the party (or coalition of parties) that wins the majority of constituencies is elected into government, and the losing parties often have no representation in government. The strength of PR systems lies in reflecting the votes cast in those elected, while FPTP systems tend to lead to more decisive outcomes.

A

Elections alone are not enough to guarantee there is genuine competition for power. Many non-democratic countries hold elections. For example, there are elections in China at various levels. However, it is the Communist Party of China that decides which candidates are allowed to enter the ballot, which means that in reality voters have a restricted choice.

Therefore, a core principle of democratic systems is that elections are free and fair. This enables all adult citizens in a society to register to vote, and to vote freely, in secret, for the political candidate of their choice without fear or intimidation. In addition, registered political parties and candidates have equal rights to contest the elections, may hold rallies and meetings, and may campaign for people to vote for them.

A fair election means that the results of the election accurately reflect how people voted.

A   Mahant Bharatdas
    Darshandas is the only
    voter in the Gir forest
    in the Indian state of
    Gujarat. India's electoral
    rules state that no citizen
    should have to travel more
    than 2 kilometres to reach
    a voting booth, so each
    year a polling team travels
    35 kilometres to ensure
    that Darshandas can cast
    his vote in a makeshift
    cardboard polling booth
    at Banej.
B   A crowd watches Sean
    'P Diddy' Combs at a
    'Vote or Die' rally in 2004
    in Miami. The 'Vote or Die'
    campaign, backed by
    a number of celebrities,
    aimed to get young
    people in the USA
    to turn out and vote.

But in many authoritarian countries, elections are held to increase the legitimacy of the ruling regime. Political opponents are often locked up or harassed by security forces on the orders of the government, political parties are frequently banned or prevented from campaigning, and elections are rigged to ensure the ruling party wins. Such elections are not free and fair, because only the ruling party has a realistic chance of winning the election and entering government.

B

A

Political parties are essential institutions in a democracy.

By competing in elections, they ensure that citizens have a choice as to how and by whom they are governed. Political parties offer this choice because they represent a range of different political ideologies and perspectives. Consequently, they help to guarantee pluralism in society. Some parties have socialist leanings, others emphasize liberalism or conservatism, and some prioritize environmental protection. When in opposition, political parties also play a crucial role in holding governments to account.

A Balochistan Nationalist Party (BNP) supporters shout slogans during a protest against alleged vote rigging in Quetta, May 2013. High turnout in Pakistan's landmark election was a positive step for democracy despite the fact the campaign was marred by violence and irregularities.

B A fundamental principle of democracies is that anyone can stand to be an elected representative. This was put into practice by English musician Screaming Lord Sutch, founder of the satirical Official Monster Raving Loony Party, who stood in over 40 elections.

B

The second key element of a democratic system is that citizens actively participate in politics and civic life. This is essential to promote the culture of democracy to which Alexis de Tocqueville referred (see Chapter 1). This means that people have a responsibility to be informed about public matters, to know how the government is using its powers, and to express their opinions and preferences on various issues.

As previously mentioned, one of the most important civic duties is for people to vote in elections. For democracies to function effectively, it is important that citizens fully understand the views and policy positions of different political parties and candidates, and vote based on this understanding.

A

B

To be able to make an informed decision when voting, citizens need to have information about politics and government policies in their country.

For most people, this means reading newspapers or websites with news stories, and also watching the news on TV. Therefore, an independent media – that is, not controlled by the government – is fundamental to democratic systems. A free press provides people with information about issues in their country, what the government is doing to address any problems, and what effects policies may have. In doing so, the media helps to ensure that governments are accountable and transparent.

In many non-democratic countries, there are significant restrictions on the media and on the flow of information in society. According to the democracy watchdog Freedom House, 45% of countries in the world had media environments that were 'not free' in 2017, in which the media was either fully controlled or heavily censored by governments. Turkmenistan, North Korea and Uzbekistan were the countries with the least press freedom.

Participation in politics and civil life in democracies means more than just voting in elections.

People should be able to join a political party and stand for office. They should be allowed to discuss and debate public issues freely, and to criticize the government. They should also be able to petition the government and other political representatives on public issues. Peaceful protests should be permitted in order to bring about change. If you live in a democratic country, you have probably been asked to donate money or to sign a petition by members of an organization representing a particular cause. You may even have set up one yourself. These organizations are part of civil society, and having an independent civil society is fundamental to the functioning of a democracy.

A   Civil society organizations provide a link between elected representatives and the general public. Their activities include running public campaigns to raise public awareness, such as this one by Amnesty International calling for an end to the use of child soldiers.

B   Citizens engaging with politics and protesting peacefully is one of the key aspects of democracy. Civil society organizations, such as Amnesty International, often seek to engage and mobilize the public to act on political issues, such as protecting human rights.

C   Civil society groups often inform and influence government policies through public consultation meetings. This photograph shows a public consultation process in Myanmar in 2017 on the National Consultation on the Draft Guideline on Public Participation in Environmental Impact Assessment.

Freedom House is a US-based non-governmental organization (NGO) founded in 1941 that conducts research and advocacy on democracy, political freedom and human rights. Its annual report is considered one of the leading assessments of the state of democracy and human rights across the world.

Censorship refers to the suppression of speech, ideas and other information by governments or private pressure groups because the material is considered obscene, politically unacceptable or a threat to security.

C

Civil society movements have often been catalysts for democratization. However, the role of civil society does not end with putting democracy in place. A free and active civil society is a crucial part of democracy, and a key function of civil society is to inform and influence policy-making. Civil society organizations encompass a wide range of issues and beliefs. They represent the interests of various professions and businesses, as well as those of trade unions, which seek to promote the rights of workers in a particular sector. Civil society organizations may also represent diverse religious views and political perspectives. Therefore, like political parties, civil society helps to ensure that different opinions in society are identified and respected.

One of the most important roles that civil society plays is to ensure that the basic rights of individuals are promoted and protected.

This may mean a focus on protecting the rights of specific groups, such as women, children, ethnic minorities and sexual minorities.

A

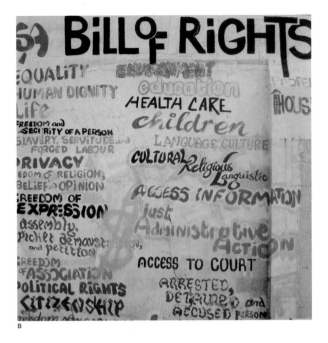

The third key element of a democratic system is the protection of individual rights. Many of these are incorporated into the Universal Declaration of Human Rights, as described in Chapter 1. These basic entitlements include the right to your own beliefs, to freedom of speech and association, to travel within and out of your country, and to practise your own religion and culture – even if you are a minority group. They also include the right to criticize and to protest government actions. As long as citizens exercise these rights peacefully and without infringing on those of others, the government cannot take them away – even if a majority of people in a country support the government.

This is perhaps the most contentious element of Diamond's definition of democracy. However, the protection of individual rights is often the most visible difference between democratic and non-democratic systems. In many autocracies, individual rights such as free speech are heavily restricted. In fact, in many dictatorships, a book such as this, which discusses politics and criticizes governments, would be censored or even banned.

The protection of individual rights is essential for other parts of the democratic system to function, too. For citizens to be able to vote in a meaningful way, for example, they have to be allowed to access information and to discuss their opinions freely. To take part in political and civil life, people must be free to speak out on different issues, to join political parties or civil society organizations, and to protest peacefully.

A

64 CHAPTER 2

B

Whereas some basic rights, such as freedom of speech, are viewed as essential to all democracies, others are more contested and may vary across different countries. For example, capital punishment is seen as a violation of human rights in some democracies, such as those in the European Union, but not in others, including in parts of the USA or India. Economic rights, such as the provision of food and healthcare, often receive less attention and protection in many democratic countries.

A   On the left is an uncensored edition of the *International New York Times* from 1 December 2015. On the right, the story about the economic problems in Thailand has been removed by the Thai government and replaced by a message from the editors stating they had nothing to do with the story's removal.

B   Public debate has occurred in Hyde Park, London, since the 1860s. Addressing crowds at Speakers' Corner, Communist MP Shapurji Saklatvala calls for the release of the Reichstag fire suspects in Germany in 1933.

C   A speaker standing on a milk crate, with a sign advocating free speech, addresses a crowd at Speakers' Corner in 1993. The right to free speech is fundamental to democracy.

C

The fourth key element of democratic systems is the presence of the rule of law. Political leaders and governments in a democracy must rule according to the laws that have been agreed; they cannot act outside of these laws. Democracy is a system based on the rule of law and not on the arbitrary decisions of rulers, as in monarchies or dictatorships. The rule of law is crucial for placing limits on the power of governments, maintaining order in society and protecting the rights of individuals.

Checks and balances refer to a principle of government in which the separate branches of government – the legislative, the executive and the judiciary – are provided with the power to prevent actions by other branches. The specific form checks and balances take differs across different countries and systems. In the US presidential system, checks and balances include the president (in the executive branch) being able to veto laws made by the legislature, or the judiciary declaring laws to be unconstitutional. Checks and balances ensure that no single branch of government becomes too powerful.

Equality before the law

Checks and balances on the use of power by individuals and governments

Right to silence

Presumption of innocence

Fair trial and independence of the judiciary

Right to assemble

Democracy through formal legal processes

Access to justice

Freedom of speech/media

A

A The rule of law can be viewed as a hierarchy of principles. At the top is the principle that everyone is equal before the law. At the next level are checks and balances on government and individuals' power. This is followed by principles that address issues of arrest and detention, including the right to silence, the presumption of innocence and the right to a fair trial. The bottom level deals with basic individual rights that are crucial to the rule of law, such as the right to freedom of speech.

B A meeting of the Italian Supreme Court in 2014. The Supreme Court is usually the highest court within a country's legal system. It plays a crucial role in upholding the rule of law in the democratic system.

B

In addition, the rule of law means that all citizens must be treated as equal before the law and cannot be discriminated against on the basis of race, ethnicity, gender or religion. The government cannot arbitrarily arrest or imprison citizens. If you are detained, you have the right to know what are the charges against you, and you have the right to a fair and public trial by an impartial court.

Within constitutional democracies, the rule of law is typically based on a separation of powers between three parts of government: the legislature that makes the law, the executive that executes or administers the law, and the judiciary that ensures the law is followed. In this way, each part of government provides checks and balances on the other parts.

A   In Brown v. Board of Education in 1954, the Supreme Court ruled that state laws establishing separate public schools for black and white children in the USA were unconstitutional. This was a huge verdict for the Civil Rights Movement, helping to end segregation in the USA.

B   This front cover of an *Extra* edition of the *New York Post* on 8 August 1974 announces US President Richard Nixon's resignation as a result of the Watergate scandal.

C   British newscaster David Frost interviews former US President Nixon in April 1977. Nixon famously claimed: 'if the President does it, it's not illegal' – a statement that runs contrary to the rule of law.

A

An independent judiciary is one of the most critical institutions in the democratic system. The judiciary is the court system responsible for ensuring that government actions are in accordance with the rule of law. It also settles disputes between the state and individuals, and plays a crucial role in promoting and protecting rights in democratic countries.

The rule of law in democratic states places significant limits on government power. In a democracy, no one – including the leader of the country – is above the law. Leaders that break the law are usually removed from office. A notorious example of this is the Watergate scandal in the 1970s, which led to impeachment proceedings being launched against US President Richard Nixon, prompting his resignation.

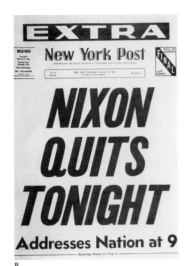

EXTRA

New York Post

NIXON QUITS TONIGHT

Addresses Nation at 9

B

The **Watergate scandal** was a political scandal in the USA in the early 1970s. It centred around a break-in at the Democratic National Committee headquarters in the Watergate office complex in 1972. President Nixon tried to cover up his involvement, which led to a constitutional crisis. An investigation uncovered multiple abuses of power. Nixon was forced to resign and many in his administration were indicted.

Richard Nixon (1913–94) was the president of the USA between 1969 and 1974. Soon after his landslide victory against George McGovern in the 1972 elections, details of the Watergate scandal began to emerge. He subsequently resigned from the presidency in 1974, making him the first president in US history to do so.

There are differences in how democratic systems limit government power. The US presidential system has been set up to include checks and balances that significantly limit executive power. Power is split between the president and Congress; it is decentralized among states and local governments, and the judiciary can overturn laws on constitutional grounds. By contrast, in the British parliamentary system, there are far fewer checks and balances. There is no written constitution and no federal system, and the first-past-the-post voting system has until recently tended to mean that the government usually has a strong legislative majority, enabling it to pass legislation more easily.

C

So, is democracy the most effective form of government there has ever been? How do these different parts of the democratic system work together to create an effective government? And what are the major benefits for people living in democracies?

A   This photograph taken in May 1945 shows emaciated survivors at Ebensee in Austria, one of the biggest Nazi concentration camps. The genocide committed by the Nazi regime saw the murder of 6 million Jews.
B   Between 1975 and 1979, thousands were imprisoned by the brutal Khmer Rouge regime at Tuol Sleng prison, Phnom Penh, Cambodia, where they faced extreme torture and execution. Around 1.5 to 3 million people were killed during the Cambodian genocide.

A

One of the most important benefits of democracy is that it provides people with more freedom than any other form of government. This is because democratic governments restrict the power of leaders, dependent as they are on the continual support of their citizens, thus preventing tyranny. By definition, democracies have greater respect for people's basic human rights than is seen in a dictatorship.

This means that democracies have avoided the atrocities associated with some dictatorships, such as the Holocaust that was carried out under the Nazi regime.

In totalitarian dictatorships, it is not only in the fields of politics and government that people have no say; these regimes control all aspects of their citizens' public and private lives, including the economy, education, art, science and morality. This can be seen in Hitler's Germany, the Soviet Union under Stalin and modern-day North Korea. One of the more absurd examples of this control is Turkmen leader Saparmurat Niyazov's decision to rename days and months in Turkmenistan after himself and his family members.

> Even beyond these extreme cases, democracies provide greater individual freedom than non-democratic systems. People are free to publicly criticize the government in democracies, they can choose what to read and where to get their information, and they can decide what they want to believe and with whom they want to associate.

Joseph Stalin (1879–1953) was a Soviet revolutionary and leader. He ruled the Soviet Union as a dictator from the mid-1920s until his death in 1953. He led the Soviet Union during World War II, playing a key role in the defeat of Germany. Stalin's rule is associated with totalitarianism, extensive political repression and mass killings.

Saparmurat Niyazov (1940–2006) was the president of Turkmenistan from its independence in 1990 until his death in 2006. Prior to this, he was First Secretary of the Turkmen Communist Party within the Soviet Union. He was widely seen as one of the world's most totalitarian and repressive dictators.

A

B

C

D

In short, democracy provides individuals with more opportunity to live their lives as they wish.

Democracy is also linked to greater prosperity for citizens. The wealthiest countries in the world tend to be democratic, although whether this is because democracy leads to economic development or because economic development promotes democracy is debatable.

A Franz Kafka's *The Trial* (1925) tells the story of a man arrested on unnamed charges. It provides a critique of bureaucracy combined with totalitarianism.

B Aldous Huxley's *Brave New World* (1932) is a dystopian novel, depicting a future with a World State run by tyrants who use brainwashing to bring about conformity.

C George Orwell's *1984* (1949) presents a future in which omnipresent government surveillance is used to persecute individualism.

D Saparmurat Niyazov established a cult of personality in Turkmenistan that included building gold statues of himself, banning ballet and opera performances, making it illegal for men to listen to car radios, and banning young men from having beards or long hair. These examples demonstrate the pervasive control that his regime had over people's lives. Niyazov was also considered to be one of the world's worst violators of human rights.

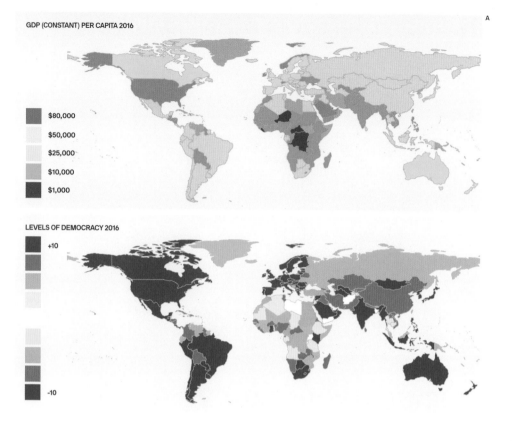

GDP (CONSTANT) PER CAPITA 2016

$80,000
$50,000
$25,000
$10,000
$1,000

LEVELS OF DEMOCRACY 2016

+10

-10

A The world map that shows levels of
   GDP per capita in 2016 (top) is strikingly
   similar to the map that shows levels
   of democracy in 2016, scored between
   -10 (least democratic) and +10 (most
   democratic) on the Polity IV index
   (bottom). On the whole, the richest
   countries are also the most democratic.
   Some believe that this is because
   democracy is best supported in wealthier
   countries; others argue it is because
   democracy leads to economic growth.

B The ruins of Mobutu's once lavish palace
   in Gbadolite, Democratic Republic of
   the Congo. Mobutu was the archetypal
   corrupt dictator, using national resources
   to enrich himself while most citizens
   endured severe poverty.

C Mobutu spent millions on the palace
   and international airport in Gbadolite,
   which were pillaged after he fled the
   country in 1997. The abandoned and
   decaying buildings are a symbol of
   the excesses of his totalitarian rule.

However, several very influential economists, including Nobel Prize winner Douglass North, argue that a country's political institutions are the most important factor in determining its economic development; specifically, countries with more democratic institutions experience more sustained economic growth than those with autocratic institutions. There is a variety of ways in which democracy supports sustained economic development.

By limiting the power of political elites, democratic systems prevent the high-level corruption that so often undermines economic development.

There are countless examples of corrupt dictators stealing their country's wealth for private use. Perhaps the most notorious is Mobutu Sese Seko, the former military ruler of Zaire (now the Democratic Republic of the Congo), who embezzled up to $15 billion of the country's wealth and flew on Concorde for shopping sprees in Paris while the majority of those in Zaire lived in extreme poverty. Institutions promoting accountability and transparency in democracies prevent such abuses of power.

The rule of law and protection of individual rights in democracies ensure that property rights are protected, which many see as the key determinant of economic growth. Secure property rights mean that people can profit from their investment and efforts, which subsequently provides incentives for further investment and fosters competition. The protection of individual rights and the freer flow of information in democracies promote creativity and entrepreneurship, which drive economic progress. In short, democracy is seen as the best form of government in which market capitalism can flourish, and this in turn promotes prosperity.

B

Douglass North (1920–2015) was a US economist and a pioneer in institutional economics. He was awarded the Nobel Prize in Economic Sciences in 1993 for his application of economic theory and quantitative methods to economic history to understand economic and institutional change.

C

Mobutu Sese Seko (1930–97) was the military dictator and president of the Democratic Republic of the Congo (which he renamed Zaire) between 1965 and 1997. He came to power with the support of Belgian forces in a *coup d'état*. Mobutu is widely seen as an archetypal dictator; he established highly autocratic rule and a cult of personality, and also amassed a personal fortune.

Public goods are services or commodities that can be consumed by an individual without reducing their availability to another, and from which no one can be excluded. They provide a benefit for society as a whole rather than for one individual.

Amartya Sen (b. 1933) is an Indian economist and philosopher. He is currently the Thomas W. Lamont Professor at Harvard University. He won the Nobel Prize in Economic Sciences in 1998 for his work in welfare economics.

Haile Selassie (1892–1975) was the emperor of Ethiopia from 1930 to 1974, and before this he was Ethiopia's regent between 1916 and 1930. He ruled Ethiopia with absolute power until he was overthrown in a *coup d'état* in 1974.

In addition, democracy ensures that governments have a greater incentive to provide public goods, such as national defence and clean air, with wider interpretations including services such as education and law enforcement, and to implement policies that improve well-being in society. If they fail to do this, they risk being voted out of office at the next election. This has meant that democracies tend to spend more on public goods than non-democracies.

The media and civil society organizations ensure that such issues receive public attention, which helps to promote greater government accountability.

Despite the disagreement about whether democracy causes economic growth or economic growth leads to democracy, it is generally accepted that democracies have avoided the worst-case scenarios of economic development. They do not feature among the poorest countries in the world.

A

A   Instead of taking steps to address the major famine that occurred in Ethiopia in 1973, Emperor Haile Selassie tried to cover it up. The absence of a free press in the country meant many were not aware that a devastating famine was taking place. The British television presenter Jonathan Dimbleby and his news team managed to gain access to Ethiopia and produced a documentary titled *The Unknown Famine*, which alerted many Ethiopians, as well as the rest of the world, to what was going on. The news report led to protests and unrest in Ethiopia, which resulted in the downfall of Selassie. However, another devastating famine occurred in the 1980s under the autocratic regime that replaced him. In contrast, no established democracy has experienced such famines.

B   In 1984 many children suffered from starvation because of food shortages during the war in Ethiopia. Around 1 million people died as a result of the famine, yet the government did little in response. One reason such famines do not occur in democracies is because political leaders have strong incentives to prevent such crises.

B

In fact, no famine has ever occurred in a functioning democracy. This is a key finding of another Nobel Prize-winning economist, Amartya Sen, in his work on famines. Sen argues that famines tend to occur in autocracies, such as in Bengal under British rule in the 1940s, in China in the late 1950s as a result of the Great Leap Forward, and famously in Ethiopia in the 1970s, under the rule of Emperor Haile Selassie and again in the 1980s under the Derg regime. This is because famines are caused by the poor distribution of food due to governance failings rather than by insufficient food availability. In democracies, there are strong incentives for political leaders to avoid such crises, which, combined with a free press, ensure that famine is prevented.

Democracy can provide greater domestic peace and stability, and there are several characteristics that help to avoid internal conflicts.

A French President François Mitterrand and German Chancellor Helmut Kohl meet at the Douaumont cemetery in 1984. After long periods of conflict between the two nations, it would now be almost unthinkable for France and Germany to go to war. Many people put this down to the two countries being established democracies.

B This political artwork by Filippo Minelli is located in Nouakchott, Mauritania. In 2008, a week after he painted 'democracy' onto the decrepit boat, Mauritanian army generals overthrew the democratically elected Mauritanian President Abdallahi in a *coup d'état*.

A

Democratic systems offer different groups in society the opportunity to participate in political processes and to have their grievances heard. This reduces the risk of such groups turning to violence to achieve their objectives. By promoting accountability, democratic systems make sure that governments address the concerns of different groups. As previously mentioned, a core part of democracy is putting restrictions on government power, which means that governments cannot easily violate the rights of different groups in society, thus reducing the likelihood of these groups taking up arms against those in power.

This has meant that functioning democracies have managed to avoid falling into the conflict traps that many other countries, such as Angola and Mozambique, have experienced, where civil wars occur repeatedly and destroy lives and livelihoods. In countries that have experienced bloody civil wars, such as Guinea and Liberia, transitions to democracy have helped to promote peace.

In addition to promoting peace within countries, democracy is linked to international peace. No war has ever occurred between established democracies. This is one of the most important findings in international relations and provides support for the democratic peace theory. The origins of this theory are in the work of German political philosopher Immanuel Kant, who argued that an international system of republics would see less war, as the majority of people would never vote to go to war unless in self-defence. Therefore, if all countries were representative democracies, no country would start a war.

Proponents of the democratic peace theory offer a number of explanations for why democracies do not go to war with other democracies. This includes leaders being accountable to the voting public for the losses that occur as a result of war, democracies not viewing other democracies as being hostile, and governments that are accountable to the public being more inclined to set up diplomatic channels to resolve tensions.

B

3. The Limits of Democracy

There are significant limits to how democracy functions in practice.

In part, this is because there are tensions and contradictions between the different aspects of the democratic system. It is also because there is a range of political, economic and social factors that affect the way democracy works. Since democracy emerged, many have cast doubt on whether it really is the most effective form of government. Others have questioned the extent to which democracy actually differs from other forms of government.

A major tension at the heart of representative democracy is the relationship between citizens and elected representatives. Although it is the people that rule in democracies, their power is entrusted to elected representatives who govern on their behalf, supposedly in accordance with their interests.

A There are serious concerns about the impact on democratic politics of the huge sums of money involved in campaign finance. In the USA, this has led to a movement called Democracy Spring, which looks to end big money in politics.

B The political influence of media moguls, such as Rupert Murdoch, has led to growing concerns about the weakening of democracy. David Cameron (left) and Jeremy Hunt (right) are 'controlled' by Murdoch at the launch of the campaign group Hacked Off in July 2011.

B

Joseph Schumpeter (1883–1950) was an Austrian-born US economist and political scientist. He spent most of his career at Harvard University and was one of the most influential economists of the 20th century.

Oligarchy is a political system in which power lies with a small number of people, who are generally among the wealthiest in society.

News Corp was a US multinational mass media corporation founded in 1978 by the Australian-born US billionaire Rupert Murdoch. Its holdings included newspapers, magazines and TV companies across the world. In 2014, its major holding were split into successor companies.

Yet despite the great promise of democracy as government by the people and for the people, many question the extent to which elected officials represent the will of the people. Most democracies are characterized by great inequalities of power between elites and the rest of society. Given these inequalities, how much choice and influence do citizens actually have? According to the economic theorist Joseph Schumpeter, 'Democracy means only that the people have the opportunity of accepting or refusing the men who are to rule them.'

In most democracies, big businesses and lobby groups representing powerful economic interests exert a huge influence on politics – often to the detriment of the majority of citizens. An influential study in 2014 looking at public policy issues in the USA between 1981 and 2002 found that economic elites and organized groups representing business interests have a substantial impact on US government policy, whereas average citizens and mass-based interest groups have little or no independent influence on policy. The implication is that the USA is actually more of an oligarchy than a democracy.

Big businesses also have significant control over the flow of information in society. Most mainstream media sources are part of larger corporations that have clear business interests, which are often promoted through their framing of political news. The potential to influence public opinion significantly has meant global media corporations, such as News Corp, have a huge influence on politics in democratic countries.

A

A fundamental principle of democracy is that any citizen is free to run for political office. This helps ensure that government is not dominated by hereditary elites, as in an aristocracy. However, the costs of running an effective election campaign are often so high that powerful backing is essential to have any chance of winning high-level political office. In the 2016 US presidential elections, both main candidates – Hillary Clinton and Donald Trump – spent more than $250 million on their campaigns. The vast sums of money needed to run an effective campaign enable big businesses to influence democratic politics.

In many democratic countries, elected officials are far from representative of the general public, coming instead from highly privileged backgrounds. For example, more than half of the ministers in British Prime Minister David Cameron's Cabinet in 2014 attended elite fee-paying schools, and half attended Oxford or Cambridge University. Many questioned how these ministers could truly represent ordinary people in Britain, given that most had never experienced the problems that the majority of people face.

The lack of diversity in socioeconomic backgrounds is not the only flaw.

Women remain significantly under-represented in politics in the majority of democracies around the world. Bolivia and Rwanda are the only two countries where women have more seats than men in parliament. Globally, women hold less than a quarter of all seats in parliament, and those that are in political office often face sexism and misogyny. The situation is worse in high political office: the USA, for example, has never had a female president.

Hillary Clinton (b. 1947) is a US politician who was Secretary of State between 2009 and 2013, senator for New York between 2001 and 2009, and First Lady of the USA between 1993 and 2001. She was the Democratic Party's nominee for president in the 2016 elections.

David Cameron (b. 1966) is a British politician who was prime minister between 2010 and 2016, and leader of the Conservative Party between 2005 and 2016. He resigned as prime minister after Britain voted to leave the European Union in the referendum he called.

A More than $600 million was spent on the Trump campaign in the 2016 US elections, and close to $1.2 billion was spent on Clinton's campaign. These huge sums of money negatively impact democracy. It means that high-level politics is dominated by elites, and government is less representative. It also gives big business and other donors excessive influence in politics.

B Australian Prime Minister Julia Gillard delivered a parliamentary speech in October 2012 describing the sexism and misogyny of opposition leader Tony Abbott. The 'misogyny speech', which went viral on the Internet, has had a huge impact on drawing attention to sexism.

A

The huge inequalities in power in most democracies are inherently tied to the vast economic inequalities that we see around the world.

The large and increasing inequality between the rich and poor is the biggest obstacle to the effective functioning of democratic systems. Indeed, it has long been recognized in developing nations that inequality can negatively impact democracy in different ways.

Clientelism refers to the exchange of goods and services for political support. It generally involves asymmetric relations between political actors (patrons) and members of the public (clients), and is considered a form of corruption. It can also undermine democratic processes by stifling political competition.

Inequality traps refer to persistent differences in wealth, power and social status that remain over time and across generations to prevent the poor from upward mobility and the rich from downward mobility. They are typically reinforced by economic, political and social structures.

B

A Papwa Sewgolum Municipal Golf Course sits next to a sprawling informal settlement in Durban, South Africa. The huge divide between rich and poor shown in the photograph exists in many countries around the world, and is the biggest factor undermining the functioning of democracy. High inequality prevents citizens from having an equal say in how their countries are governed.

B The sight of an impoverished slum next to modern skyscrapers, seen here in Luanda, Angola, is now commonplace in many countries. The huge gap between rich and poor looks set to increase in most nations, posing a significant threat to democratic processes. High economic inequality leads to skewed public policies that favour the wealthy and harm those worst off in society.

During elections, candidates may capture votes through clientelism. Wealthier groups can then use their resources to influence politicians to implement policies that are skewed towards the rich. Greater access to resources allows the rich to prevail in open disputes and wealthier groups also frequently prevent issues from being discussed. Sometimes, poorer groups that are unable to get their concerns recognized on the political agenda abandon their attempts to influence policy.

This relationship between economic inequality and unequal power and influence is sustained over time through various mechanisms and institutions creating inequality traps.

The negative effect of high levels of economic inequality on democratic processes is not restricted to developing countries.

A

B

In wealthy democracies, the high levels of economic inequality are linked to policy outcomes that favour the rich and disadvantage the poor. This has led to the problem of social exclusion. High inequality fuels discontent and is linked to instability in democratic systems. It is also a major barrier to political participation.

The idea that politics serves the interests of elites leads people to feel disillusioned and disengaged with democratic politics.

As discussed in Chapter 2, citizen engagement is not only a basic element of democratic systems, but it is also crucial for other elements of democratic systems, and for the functioning of democracy more generally.

The influential political scientist Robert Putnam examines the problem of public apathy in *Bowling Alone* (2000). He discusses how citizen disengagement with politics in the USA has led to a decrease in voter turnout, attendance at public meetings and membership of political parties.

This, Putnam argues, is the result of declining social capital in the country. Falling membership in civic organizations, such as religious groups and labour unions, and lower in-person social activity more generally have eroded social capital. Putnam points to the rise of technology, such as TV and the Internet, as being a key factor, because people spend far more of their leisure time alone.

Public disengagement with democratic politics can provide fertile ground for the growth of populism.

Robert Putnam (b. 1941) is a US political scientist and Malkin Professor of Public Policy at the Harvard University John F. Kennedy School. He is known for his work on the relationship between social capital and democracy.

Social capital refers to the networks of relations between people in a society based on reciprocity, trust and cooperation that enable a society to function effectively.

A   A protester holds up a placard reading 'Remove Corruption Retain Subsidy!' at Gani Fawehinmi Park, Lagos, in 2012. The protest was against President Jonathan's government decision to scrap a fuel subsidy.

B   Demonstrations were held in Lagos against soaring petrol prices in 2012. Many Nigerians felt that cheap fuel was the only benefit they got from the country's oil wealth.

C   Music on. World off. Some feel that disengagement with democratic politics is linked to technology, such as the digital audio player, which enables people to spend more of their leisure time alone.

D   Putnam argues that the shift away from group-based activities has led to a decline in social capital, and less engagement with democracy.

This involves a form of politics in which charismatic leaders are able to arouse a group of people that feel marginalized by mainstream politics. In turn, this perceived marginalization enables these leaders to pit 'ordinary people' against 'the establishment'. Populism promotes a form of politics reliant on appeals to emotional impulses, often rooted in people's fears rather than reasoned debate and evidence. As well as being opposed to political elites, populism is frequently based on the vilification of minority groups in a society. This can be seen in Trump's election campaign, when he called Mexican migrants in the USA 'criminals' and 'rapists', and pledged to ban Muslims from entering the USA.

The danger of populism highlights another important tension in democracy.

A   A cyclist swears at London Mayor Boris Johnson in 2015. There is growing frustration with politicians in many democracies.
B   The satirical carnival float at the Rose Monday parade in Düsseldorf, Germany, in 2017 compares US President Donald Trump, French far-right leader Marine Le Pen and Dutch MP Geert Wilders with Adolf Hitler.

James Madison (1751–1836) was one of the Founding Fathers of the United States, and was US president from 1809 to 1817. He played a key role in drafting the US Constitution and the Bill of Rights.

Modernization theory considers the process of transition that nations go through as they move from traditional societies to modern ones.

Seymour Martin Lipset (1922–2006) was a US political sociologist who held positions at Stanford University, George Mason University and Harvard University. He is considered one of the leading theorists of democracy in the 20th century.

A

Adam Przeworski (b. 1940) is a Polish-American political scientist. He is currently a professor of political science at New York University. He is considered one of the most important theorists of democracy and political economy.

Democracy is built on the idea that the people are the ultimate authority in society, and that popular participation is essential to politics. But what if the majority of people in a country decide to violate the human rights of other people in society – or they decide to support a leader who disregards the rule of law?

As far back as the emergence of democracy in ancient Athens, critics of the system have argued that it leads to mob rule. US President James Madison was particularly critical of democracy because of the potential for the majority rule in society to restrict individual liberties. The checks and balances built into democratic institutions have often been designed to prevent this tyranny of the majority, as well as to limit the power of government.

Modernization theorists, such as Seymour Martin Lipset, have argued that there has to be very little poverty in a society to ensure that people do not succumb to the appeals of demagogues. Therefore, for democracy to survive, a country needs to have a certain level of wealth. Empirical evidence from Adam Przeworski and colleagues provides support for this argument. They find that democracy has never failed in a country with a gross domestic product per capita of more than $6,055 (based on 1985 US dollar rates).

A

B

The view that a minimum level of economic development helps sustain democracy would appear to contradict the claim that democracy has led to economic development. In fact, many question whether democracy is the best system for promoting economic growth.

As discussed in Chapter 2, democracies have avoided being among the worst-case scenarios of economic development. However, they are not the best performers either. The East Asian 'Tigers' of Hong Kong, Singapore, South Korea and Taiwan provide clear examples of how authoritarian regimes may be better placed to deliver economic development. These states achieved exceptionally high rates of economic growth between the 1950s and 1990s through the close involvement of authoritarian governments in the market.

General Park Chung-hee (1917–79) was a Korean politician and general who served as the president of South Korea from 1963 until his assassination in 1979.

Lee Kuan Yew (1923–2015) was the first prime minister of Singapore and is considered to be the founding father of the country. He ruled Singapore for three decades between 1959 and 1990.

A Seoul in the 1950s. For many, South Korea's transformation is the biggest economic development success story in history. However, it took place under a dictatorship, not a democracy. Some argue this demonstrates that autocracies are better able to deliver development.

B Seoul in the present day. South Korea is now one of the world's wealthiest countries. In the 1980s, following mass protests, the country adopted a democratic system. Some argue the Korean case shows that democracy requires a minimum level of economic development.

The case of South Korea is arguably the greatest success story of economic development the world has ever seen. In a single generation, the country went from being one of the poorest countries in the world to one of the richest. This transformation occurred under the authoritarian rule of General Park Chung-hee, whose government implemented various economic measures to promote rapid industrialization and export-led growth. This included mobilizing resources to invest in key sectors, providing subsidies and loans for companies competing in global markets, strategically using tariffs and exchange rates, and keeping labour costs low – often using repressive means.

The East Asian experience has led many, including the former Singaporean leader Lee Kuan Yew, to argue that dictatorships are better placed to deliver economic growth than democracies. There are several arguments for why this might be the case.

First, dictatorships may be better at using a country's resources for productive activities that promote economic growth. Democratic governments have to meet the immediate demands of voters in order to stay in power, and so are compelled to use resources quickly. Dictatorships do not face such short-term pressures to spend and can therefore make the longer term investments needed for economic growth.

Second, dictatorships have more autonomy than democratic governments. This means they can resist the pressures of special interests, such as big business, labour unions or different socioeconomic classes.

This independence from special interests enables dictatorships to implement policies that increase economic output in society rather than serving narrow group interests.

Third, democracies are viewed as being worse at implementing reforms that promote economic development, not only because democratic governments face pressure from different groups in society that may oppose reform, but also because the various parts of the democratic system – such as legislative procedures, institutionalized checks and balances, and the representation of different interests – make rapid economic reform far more difficult to put into practice.

A

A   In many poorer countries, such as Nigeria, elections often lead to outbreaks of violence. Some argue that the competition for power associated with elections can lead to more violence in poorer, ethnically divided countries with weak institutions.

B   Campaign posters in Sarajevo, 2014. In ethnically divided countries, such as Bosnia and Herzegovina, elections are often fought along ethnic lines, with political parties choosing to appeal to people from a specific ethnic group rather than to the public as a whole. Non ethnic-based parties often struggle in elections.

B

These arguments for why autocracies may be better than democracies at promoting economic development are related to broader criticisms of the effectiveness of democracy.

Competition for power is fundamental to democracy; it promotes government accountability and ensures people have a choice on how their societies are governed.

However, this contestability can have adverse effects. Elections are frequently linked to instability, particularly in poorer countries. In the past decade, Burundi, Kenya and Nigeria have all experienced electoral violence. In some cases, such as in the Republic of the Congo in 1993, the fallout from elections has led to civil war.

Competition for power can lead to uncertainty and instability in richer countries, too. It can create negative incentives, whereby politicians are more concerned with securing power than addressing the problems facing society. This can lead to a more combative and partisan form of politics, which undermines the culture needed for democracy to flourish. Often parliamentary debates become opportunities for scoring political points rather than forums for genuine deliberation over the laws and policies that will improve people's lives.

This combative politics has fuelled political polarization in many democracies, which makes decision-making harder and creates instability. In the USA, the combination of polarization and the checks and balances in the system is widely viewed as preventing effective reforms from being implemented.

Political polarization can also lead to crisis.

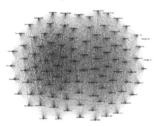

A

101st Congress, 1989 Session

For example, Belgium did not have a government between 2010 and 2011 because political parties were so divided that it took almost two years for them to reach an agreement and form a government.

A   This figure shows how political polarization has increased to an extreme level in the US House of Representatives. It indicates how over time representatives increasingly vote the same way as others in their party.
B   A Northern Irish couple who refused to provide a cake featuring a pro-gay marriage message were found guilty of discrimination in court. Yet many Christians argued that the ruling violated their religious rights and freedoms, as this meme depicts.

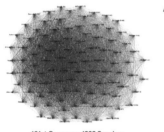

107th Congress, 2002 Session

Political polarization refers to the distance between political parties' (or groups') political preferences on various issues, and usually implies a divergence in political views.

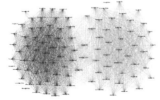

113th Congress, 2013 Session

BAKE THE CAKE

B

Another long-standing concern has been whether democracies can provide order and security. Some feel that the pluralism inherent in democracies, which allows a wide range of beliefs, combined with an emphasis on individual rights, weakens social cohesion and fuels discontent. Part of the problem is that rights are essentially contested. One person's rights to their beliefs may come into conflict with those of another.

For example, in 2014 a Christian couple in Northern Ireland who ran a bakery together refused to provide a customer with a cake decorated with a message in support of gay marriage, claiming that it contradicted their religious views. The customer filed a complaint on the grounds of discrimination, which he won. After the bakery lost its appeal against the verdict, a spokesperson claimed that the ruling undermined 'democratic freedom, religious freedom and free speech'. Some people may agree that the couple discriminated against the customer, but others feel they should be free not to do something that goes against their beliefs. Such disputes are very difficult to address in a way that does not leave some people feeling as though their rights have been violated.

Democratic governments have often placed limits on individuals' rights in the interests of national security.

In some cases, democratic governments have committed grave human rights abuses under the pretence of protecting national security. One of the starkest examples of this is the US government's internment of Japanese-Americans after the Japanese attack on Pearl Harbor during World War II. Between 110,000 and 120,000 people of Japanese ancestry – two-thirds of whom were US citizens – were forcibly relocated and incarcerated from 1942 to 1945 on the basis that they represented a security threat to the USA. An investigation by the US government years later found little evidence of this threat, and instead concluded that the flagrant violation of the civil rights was the product of racism.

A

B

A   Armed security guards patrol the Eiffel Tower on 9 January 2015, during a huge manhunt for the two suspected gunmen in the deadly attack on the offices of *Charlie Hebdo* magazine.

B   Australia's use of an offshore immigration centre in Nauru to detail migrants arriving by boat has been heavily criticized for being a gross violation of the human rights of migrants and refugees. The UN High Commissioner for Human Rights has repeatedly called for the closure of the centre due to the human rights abuses occurring there.

C   A number of high-profile cases of police killing unarmed black men in the USA spurned the Black Lives Matter movement. A man yells, 'Hands up, don't shoot,' in Ferguson, Missouri, while protesting the death of Michael Brown in August 2014.

c

More recently, there has been unease that counter-terrorist measures by democratic governments have led to rights abuses.

These measures include the anti-terror laws introduced in Britain since 2000 that allow the indefinite detention without charge of foreign nationals suspected of terrorism, pre-charge detention of up to 14 days without charge, control orders that impose severe prohibitions (such as house arrest) without charge, and the banning of non-violent political organizations.

There are many examples of democratic governments violating the rights of minority groups. This includes the mistreatment of the indigenous aboriginal population of Australia at the hands of successive governments, for which the Australian government issued a formal apology in 2008. It also includes the criminalization of homosexuality in Britain, which was not fully ended across the country until 2003. More recently, the United Nations has raised serious concerns about the rights of refugees being abused by democratic governments.

A   B

Many have questioned the notion that democracies are more peaceful than non-democracies. Indeed, a significant number of international conflicts have involved democratic countries. Often these conflicts have occurred despite public opposition to going to war. In some cases, such as the US-led invasion of Iraq in 2002, the promotion of democracy was one of the reasons stated for going to war.

Over the past few decades, there has been growing concern that the process of globalization is undermining democracy. As the world has become more interconnected, there has been a proliferation of international organizations, laws and agreements to govern the global economy.

Globalization refers to the increasing economic, political and cultural interdependence in the world. It is associated with the growing trade, investment, finance and technological flows between countries. While it is often seen as driven by technological advancement alone, it has also come about through the political decision to reduce barriers to such global flows.

Bilateral investment treaties (BITs) are agreements that establish the terms and conditions for foreign direct investment by individuals and companies from one state to another.

This has led to a shift in power from democratically elected governments to global corporations and international organizations.

In particular, the emphasis on reducing barriers to trade, finance and investment has caused many to question whether globalization has placed limits on the laws and policies democratically elected governments can introduce.

This tension between globalization and democracy is reflected in the rise of bilateral investment treaties (BITs), which have seen democratic governments being sued by global corporations for implementing policies that harm investment, even if they benefit citizens. For example, an Italian investment company sued the South African government in 2007 because its policy of trying to address the economic injustices of apartheid was obstructing investment. Although the South African government settled the case, it has since withdrawn from its BITs because they prevent the government from implementing policies that benefit society.

C

D

A This anti-Vietnam war protest poster from 1967 is by Tomi Ungerer. The controversial 'Eat' poster shows a caricature of an Asian man being force-fed the Statue of Liberty by a disembodied white arm.

B 'Choice not Chance' (1967) by Tomi Ungerer depicts an army pilot painting figures of crying Vietnamese children on his aeroplane. Strong public opposition to the Vietnam War led to much anti-war protest.

C The Oxi movement campaigned against austerity measures in Greece, which experienced a major debt crisis following the global financial crisis of 2008. Many see the imposition of austerity measures in Greece by international creditors, despite the population voting against such action, as an example of how globalization has undermined democracy.

D This 'Austerity isn't Working' cartoon from 2012 is by Steve Bell. After the global financial crisis, the British coalition government implemented austerity measures to reduce national debt, which negatively impacted the lives of many in society, particularly the most vulnerable.

Economist Dani Rodrik has argued that democracy, national sovereignty and deep global economic integration (or 'hyperglobalization') are mutually incompatible; we can combine two of the three, but it is not possible to have all three together in full. He refers to this as the 'political trilemma of the world economy'. Deep global economic integration requires an elimination of transaction costs to trade and finance across borders. However, nation states are a major cause of such costs. Therefore, the only way to have both a significantly more globalized system and democracy would be to have some kind of global federal democracy, which is unrealistic. Rodrik argues that to maintain national democratic systems, a more restricted form of globalization is required.

Global politics has harmed democracy in other ways, too.

After World War II, the geopolitics of the Cold War led to democratic governments in many countries being replaced by dictatorships. It was often Western democracies, particularly the USA, that helped to overthrow these democratically elected governments,

Dani Rodrik (b. 1957) is a Turkish economist who is a professor of international political economy at Harvard University John F. Kennedy School. He is widely considered to be one of the most important thinkers in international political economy, international economics and economic development.

National sovereignty broadly refers to the idea that independent nations that have a government that can exercise power in society and has control over its borders should have the right to exist without interference from other nations.

A

A Augusto Pinochet watches US-made bombers flying over El Bosque in 1988. The US provided considerable support to Pinochet's dictatorship in Chile.

B Chilean troops fire on La Moneda Palace in Santiago, during a coup led by Pinochet against Allende, who died in the attack.

C La Moneda Palace 30 years later. Chile returned to democracy in 1989 after Pinochet's brutal rule, which included mass human rights violations.

B

C

Patrice Lumumba (1925–61) was a leader of the Congolese independence movement and the first democratically elected prime minister of the Democratic Republic of the Congo. He was assassinated in 1961 with the involvement of the Belgian, British and US governments.

Augusto Pinochet (1915–2006) was a Chilean politician and general, whose dictatorship was marked by severe human rights violations. He was the military ruler of Chile between 1973 and 1990.

Salvador Allende (1908–73) was a Chilean physician and politician. He was the president of Chile between 1970 and 1973, and was the first Marxist to be democratically elected as president in Latin America.

Mohammad Mosaddegh (1882–1967) was the prime minister of Iran between 1951 and 1953, serving as head of a democratically elected government. After the coup, he was imprisoned and then placed under house arrest until his death.

in order to further their own political and economic interests. They then provided essential support for dictators to stay in power while the citizens of those countries suffered. While democracies may not go to war with other democracies, there are plenty of examples of democracies backing coups to overthrow other democratically elected governments around the world, and of providing support to repressive dictators.

The CIA and the Belgian government were complicit in the assassination of Patrice Lumumba, the first democratically elected leader of the Democratic Republic of the Congo in 1961. This gave rise to the brutal dictatorship of Mobutu Sese Seko, who was provided financial and military support by the US government because he was an ally in the fight against communism. In 1983, the CIA supported General Augusto Pinochet's *coup d'état* in Chile to overthrow the democratically elected president Salvador Allende. The British and US governments also backed a coup in Iran against the democratically elected government of Mohammad Mosaddegh in 1953 after he nationalized the country's oil industry, and then supported the brutal rule of the Shah of Iran.

Indira Gandhi
(1917–84) was an Indian politician and prime minister of India between 1966 and 1977, and again from 1980 until her assassination in 1984. She was the first female Indian prime minister, and the second woman to be elected head of government in a democracy.

A   Mosaddegh addresses a crowd in 1951, during the critical days of the Anglo-Iranian oil dispute.
B   Following the US-backed coup, Mosaddegh was kept under house arrest until his death in 1967.

C   Indira Gandhi appears live on Indian television on 25 June 1975 to declare a national emergency, marking the start of India's two-year period of dictatorship.

In addition to these foreign power-supported coups, there are examples of democracies collapsing. In Europe in the 1930s, fascist regimes managed to bring down nascent democracies through a combination of civil conflict and exploiting the economic turmoil of the Great Depression.

One of the most important examples of democracy failing is 'the Emergency', India's two-year period of dictatorship from 1975 to 1977. It perhaps best demonstrates how the limits of democracy can lead to its failure. Economic problems in the previous years had fuelled anti-government protests, and while this was ongoing Prime Minister Indira Gandhi was found guilty of a minor violation of electoral rules. In response, she declared a national emergency, and within days the country's democratic institutions were dismantled and a dictatorship was imposed. Civil rights were suspended, tens of thousands of political opponents were imprisoned without right to trial, and censorship was imposed. Furthermore, elections were cancelled, political parties were banned, and a series of constitutional reforms was implemented to transfer power to the prime minister.

A key question is how did Gandhi manage to do this in an established democratic system?

Part of the answer is that she had the support of the country's poor majority. They had grown increasingly frustrated by the failure of Indian politics to improve their lives. Gandhi successfully convinced them that political opponents and the country's democratic institutions were preventing her from implementing the far-reaching reforms that would transform their lives. She had also spent the previous years undermining democratic processes in the country – for example, by curbing the independence of the judiciary, bringing her supporters into key positions in the political system and increasingly using executive orders to bypass and weaken parliament.

As a result, there was almost no opposition when she imposed the Emergency.

However, the Emergency also demonstrates why democracy remains the most effective form of government we have, despite its flaws. The lack of accountability led to Gandhi implementing programmes that severely violated the human rights of the poor, who had supported her. This included the violent removal of people from a slum in Delhi, and many poorer Indians were forced to undergo sterilization in a programme limiting population growth. The outcry that followed caused Gandhi to have a change of heart and to hold elections, in which she suffered a landslide defeat because of her abuse of power.

c

A

The past decade has seen democracy come under threat around the world.

A rise in nationalist and populist politics has led to the emergence of new leaders with strong authoritarian tendencies in democratic countries who have increasingly undermined different parts of the democratic system. What is perhaps most striking about this trend is that it has occurred in various regions around the world, prompting concerns that democracy is failing globally.

Paul Kagame (b. 1957) became president of Rwanda in 2000, but has been considered the country's de facto leader since 1994. He was the commander of the rebel force that ended the Rwandan genocide of 1994.

Yoweri Museveni (b. 1944) is the current president of Uganda. He has been the country's president since 1986. He was one of the leading figures in the rebellions that ended the dictatorships of Idi Amin and Milton Obote.

Rodrigo Duterte (b. 1945) is the current president of the Philippines. He assumed office in 2016. Prior to this, he was the mayor of Davao City and was among the Philippines' longest-serving mayors, in office for more than 22 years in seven terms.

B

In Africa, leaders such as Paul Kagame and Yoweri Museveni – once seen as shining lights of democracy – have clamped down on civil and political liberties. In Rwanda, Uganda and many other countries across the continent, political opponents face harassment and physical violence.

A   Rashtriya Swayamsevak Sangh (RSS) is an Indian right-wing Hindu nationalist organization founded in 1925. It has close ties to the ruling Bharatiya Janata Party.

B   People wave Turkish national flags and pro-Erdoğan banners as they gather at Kizilay Democracy Square in Ankara during a rally in 2016 against the failed military coup on July 15.

Recep Tayyip Erdoğan (b. 1954) is the current president of Turkey and took office in 2014. Prior to this he was the prime minister of Turkey from 2003 to 2014, and mayor of Istanbul from 1994 to 1998.

Narendra Modi (b. 1950) is the current prime minister of India. He became prime minister in 2014, and prior to this he was the chief minister of Gujarat from 2001 to 2014.

Leaders such as Rodrigo Duterte, Recep Tayyip Erdoğan and Narendra Modi have all undermined democratic processes under the pretence of national security and stronger government. The election of Duterte as president of the Philippines is perhaps the most glaring example of the growing disregard for rule of law and individual rights in democratic countries: Duterte publicly sanctioned the extra-judicial killing of those suspected of involvement in the country's drug trade. This has led to more than 7,000 people being killed by police officers and vigilantes between June 2016, when Duterte was sworn in as president, and March 2017. Modi's election as prime minister of India came on the back of the right-wing Hindu nationalist movement. His election brought a crackdown on civil society organizations and universities regarded as 'anti-national' – for example, civil society organizations were prevented from accessing foreign funding and students involved in anti-government protests were arrested – while minority groups were targeted by mobs emboldened by his explicit Hindu nationalism.

A   Activists, including supporters of Reporters Without Borders and Amnesty International, hold up pictures of journalists who are currently in prison in Turkey. In many countries, the crackdown on a free press is one of the first steps towards autocracy.

B   A protester sticks leaflets reading 'Freedom for all imprisoned journalists in Turkey' on a bus window during a demonstration in Hanover, Germany, in 2017 to demand the release of German journalist Deniz Yücel.

C   After the failed coup, many journalists and political dissidents were sent to Turkey's Diyarbakir Prison, where torture is widespread.

D   The combination of Putin and Trump as the leaders of arguably the two most powerful nations in the world is for many the clearest sign that democracy is failing.

Vladimir Putin (b. 1952) is the current president of Russia. He has held office since 2012. Prior to this he was prime minister between 1999 and 2000, and again from 2008 until 2012, and president between 2000 and 2008. He was a KGB foreign intelligence office for many years before entering politics.

The Brexit referendum was a referendum on whether Britain should remain in the European Union or leave. It took place on 23 June 2016, and resulted in 52% of voters in favour of leaving and 48% in favour of remaining. The result has triggered Britain's withdrawal from the European Union.

The most dramatic decline in democracy occurred in Turkey under Erdoğan.

Following a failed coup to overthrow him in 2016, the government imposed a state of emergency, which saw tens of thousands of political opponents – including journalists, academics and staff of civil society organizations – imprisoned without trial.

#make everything
great again

D

No country in the world has imprisoned more journalists than Turkey. This prompted Freedom House, the democracy watchdog, to classify Turkey as 'not free' in 2017 for the first time.

Hopes for democracy in Russia after the collapse of the Soviet Union in the early 1990s were dashed by the rise of Vladimir Putin. Political opposition has been brutally suppressed, the independent press has been stifled, the state-run media is used to prevent dissent and the rule of law is continually flouted. The resurgence of Russia under Putin as a major force in world politics has not only increased his domestic support, but also is widely seen as having helped foster the rise of authoritarian movements across Europe. The Russian government has also been accused of interfering in the 2016 US elections to help Donald Trump's presidential campaign.

There has been a huge increase in far-right nationalist movements across Europe on the back of growing anti-immigration, and particularly anti-Muslim, sentiment.

Even in European Union member states, such as Austria, France, Greece and the Netherlands, which have long promoted democracy and individual rights, political parties linked to far-right movements have grown in popularity. In Britain, the campaign to leave the European Union in the Brexit referendum was rooted in nationalist populism and fears of immigration.

In Finland, the Czech Republic, Hungary and Poland, far-right parties have gained power since 2010. The governments of Viktor Orbán in Hungary and Jarosław Kaczyński in Poland, in particular, have restricted public gatherings, closed civil society space, strengthened government control of the media, limited the independence of the judiciary, and systematically dismantled institutional checks and balances. In both cases, the ruling parties have been able to implement these measures on the back of electoral wins that gave them parliamentary majorities. These actions are seen by many as triggering the collapse of democracy in Hungary and Poland.

Despite all of this, for many the biggest indication that something has gone wrong with the state of democracy in the world occurred in 2016, with the election of Trump as US president. The USA has long projected itself as the bastion of democracy and individual liberties around the world. Indeed, many people across the globe see the USA as the world's foremost democratic country. Trump's election has seriously tarnished this image.

A

A   For many, the election of Trump as
    US president in 2016 exposed the
    weaknesses of democracy in the USA.
B   Trump's threat to 'lock up' Hillary
    Clinton in the run-up to the 2016
    presidential elections met the
    approval of many of his supporters.
C   Trump frequently accuses media
    outlets, such as CNN, of spreading
    'fake news', while himself circulating
    false stories to enhance his support.

In fact, Trump's presidential campaign and short time in office have seen him undermine democratic processes.

B

C

His campaign was based on extreme populist politics
– from pitting his predominantly white working-class
support base against the 'corrupt' Washington establishment,
to demonizing minority groups with pledges to build a wall
along the Mexican border and to impose a travel ban on
Muslims. He has even used threats to lock up his opponent,
Hillary Clinton, as part of his strategy, and launched a
series of attacks on the press. His election campaign is
also linked to the rise of 'fake news', in which false stories
were circulated deliberately, often via social media sites,
to increase his support. This has continued since Trump
became president; in fact, a notorious example of this was
his administration exaggerating the size of the crowd that
turned up for his inauguration.

Viktor Orbán (b. 1963) is the current prime
minister of Hungary. He has been prime
minister since 2010, and previously held
the same position between 1998 and 2002.
He rose to prominence leading a pro-
democracy student movement in the 1980s.

Jarosław Kaczyński (b. 1949) is a Polish
politician and was prime minister of
Poland between 2006 and 2007. He is the
cofounder of the right-wing Law and Justice
Party, which he currently chairs. Many see
him as the de facto leader of Poland.

THE CHALLENGE TO DEMOCRACY

113

A

Trump has continued to damage the country's democratic institutions since becoming president. He has targeted the judiciary with his public criticism of judges. His vitriol against the press has led to accusations of inciting violence against journalists. He has appointed family members to key positions in his administration and used the presidency to further his personal wealth. His sacking of key officials, such as the FBI director, is widely perceived as being for personal motives. In addition, Trump has increasingly aligned himself with authoritarian world leaders, such as Duterte and Putin, while alienating democratic allies such as Canada, European Union member states and South Korea, by publicly questioning and criticizing the economic and security relations between these countries and the USA. His reluctance to directly condemn white supremacist and neo-Nazi groups following a rally in Charlottesville in 2017, which led to the murder of an anti-fascist protester, has increased concerns that Trump has provided implicit support to fascist groups, who have become emboldened by his election.

What is particularly concerning for many is that he clearly expressed his disdain for democratic processes during the election campaign. But people voted for him in spite of this – or perhaps worse, because of it. This popular support for a leader who publicly undermines democratic processes is perhaps the defining feature of this autocratic trend. Leaders such as Trump, Erdoğan, Modi and Orbán have come to power by winning elections, and with significant popular support. For their supporters, this is proof of their democratic credentials.

No border.
The EU has opened our borders

No control.
to 4,000 people every week.

B

Some have suggested that these regimes represent the emergence of a new form of 'illiberal' democracy. This is a view that leaders such as Orbán have promoted. From this perspective, it is not democracy that is under threat, but liberalism that is being rejected. It is important to consider this argument. There is a danger that beliefs and outcomes that are not consistent with a cosmopolitan liberal view of the world are unfairly labelled 'undemocratic'. For example, in the case of the Brexit referendum – why should the majority's vote to leave the European Union lead to concerns over the state of democracy?

The unease about democracy is less to do with the outcome of the referendum and more about the nature of the campaign leading up to the vote, which saw the rise of demagogues whose divisive and angry rhetoric aimed to appeal to voters' fears, insecurities and prejudices.

In addition, the populist nature of the campaigns led to misinformation and hysteria rather than a reasoned evidence-based debate on whether Britain should leave the European Union. The demonizing of politicians and minority groups contributed to the murder of the MP Jo Cox, and a surge in racist hate-crimes after the referendum result. The overall effect was to damage the democratic culture of the country.

Such divisive and populist politics is generally the problem with illiberal democratic political leaders. They claim democratic legitimacy on the basis of obtaining power through elections and portray themselves as representing the people against the liberal elite establishment.

They then use this majoritarian politics to weaken countervailing forces – the media, independent judiciaries, human rights organizations, political opponents, minority groups and others that do not share their views – and to threaten their power. However, these are all important institutions that are at the heart of democratic systems. Therefore, it is not only that illiberal democratic political leaders oppose liberalism, but also that they represent threats to democracy more broadly. They use their electoral victories and popular support to undermine the other key parts of the democratic system.

But what explains this rise in populism and the increasing number of leaders with authoritarian tendencies around the world?

There have been several developments since the millennium that have led to this new challenge to democracy.

A

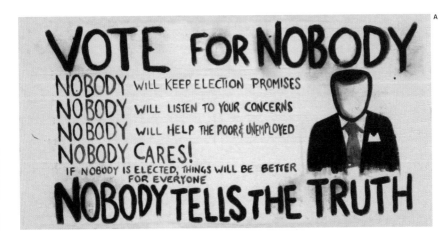

The 2008 global financial crisis is widely seen as the worst global financial crisis since the Great Depression of the 1930s. It began with a crisis in the sub-prime mortgage market in the USA and quickly became an international banking crisis, with the collapse of the investment bank Lehman Brothers in 2008. This led to a global economic downturn.

A   There is growing frustration that democracy does not serve the public's interests. Some, such as those involved in the US 'Vote for Nobody' campaign, believe people should stop voting to show their discontent.

B   This 1932 campaign poster for Adolf Hitler shows a despondent-looking crowd accompanied by the slogan, 'Our last hope Hitler'. The economic hardship of the Great Depression was central to Hitler's rise to power.

One of the most significant factors is the 2008 global financial crisis and the economic impact that this had on people throughout the world. Indeed, it is widely recognized that politics tends to take a turn to the hard right after major financial crises. The most obvious example of this is the Great Depression of the 1930s, which followed the Wall Street Crash. And the rise of fascism in Europe at that time is a key reason why many are concerned about the future of democracy following the recent financial crisis.

A

B

A   Growing economic hardship over the past decade has seen people in wealthy democracies, such as Britain and the USA, increasingly turn to food banks because they cannot afford to buy food.

B   While many struggle for basic meals, others can afford this £645 'Golden Phoenix' cupcake. The growing divide between the haves and the have-nots has fuelled discontent with the political establishment.

C   Many feel that Milanović's recent work best explains the recent rise of populism. He shows that while the real incomes of middle and working classes in developed countries have stagnated or even fallen since 1988, the incomes of the world's wealthiest and those in Asian countries have increased. This shift can be seen when we compare the composition of Asia and the West in 1988 (bottom) and 2011 (top). In Asia, the huge decline in the proportion of absolute poor has led to the shares of more affluent groups rising. This progress has not occurred in the West.

The backlash against those held responsible for the crisis has seen the majority of governments that were in power in Europe and North America at the time voted out of office. In many places, people's frustration – fuelled by economic hardship and austerity measures – has turned more broadly against the political establishment and expert knowledge. It is this frustration that has allowed populism to flourish.

The crisis laid bare huge global inequalities of wealth and income, and these have worsened since the financial crisis. A 2016 report by Oxfam found that while around 388 billion-aires owned the same amount of wealth as half the world's population in 2010, the increase in inequality means that only 62 people had the same wealth as half the world in 2016. Meanwhile, since 2010, wealthy democracies such as Britain and the USA have seen a huge rise in people turning to food banks because they are unable to afford meals. In Britain, the largest food bank network delivered around 1.2 million emergency food parcels in 2016–17. In the USA, around one in seven people (more than 45 million) rely on food banks.

This surging inequality has been driven by the process of globalization, which in part explains the rise of nationalism as the middle and working classes in developed nations have increasingly turned against the process of globalization of recent decades.

The negative impact of globalization on inequality is arguably best explained by leading economist Branko Milanović and colleagues. They show that between 1998 and 2008, although there has been a rise in real incomes of the richest in the world and of the middle class in emerging economies such as China and India, the very poorest in the world and the middle and working classes in developed nations have not gained at all. In fact, some have become worse off during this period. This is because the removal of barriers to global trade, finance and investment, together with the deregulation of national economies, can benefit some groups in society but leave others in a worse position. According to Milanović and colleagues, lower earners in developed economies such as Britain and the USA are among those who have become poorer in relative terms. For many, this trend is perhaps the biggest reason for the backlash against globalization and the discontent with democratic governance in many countries around the world.

Oxfam is an international confederation of charitable organizations that focuses on the alleviation of global poverty. It was founded in 1942 as a famine relief charity and is widely viewed as one of the leading international development NGOs in the world.

Branko Milanović (b. 1953) is a Serbian-American economist. He is currently visiting presidential professor at City University of New York and was formerly the lead economist in the World Bank's research division. He is considered one of the foremost scholars of global inequality.

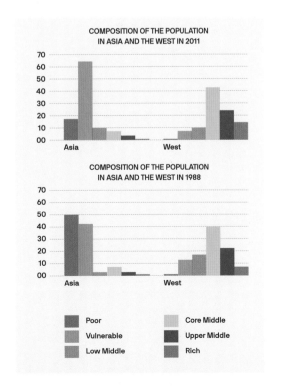

COMPOSITION OF THE POPULATION
IN ASIA AND THE WEST IN 2011

COMPOSITION OF THE POPULATION
IN ASIA AND THE WEST IN 1988

Poor   Core Middle
Vulnerable   Upper Middle
Low Middle   Rich

There is evidence to suggest that the trend towards right-wing politics after financial crises gradually peters out over time. However, there are concerns that the economic fallout from the global financial crisis of 2008 signals a far bigger threat looming for the future of democracy. The reason democracy flourished in Europe and North America after World War II is because it was able to provide citizens with significant economic security. For many, it is becoming increasingly clear that this economic security is no longer guaranteed, which means the survival of democracy is in jeopardy.

The growing security threat faced by democratic countries has also been a major factor in the rise of 'strong' authoritarian leaders.

A

JE SUIS CHARLIE

JE SUIS BRUXELLES

JE SUIS NICE

JE SUIS ORLANDO

JE SUIS MUNICH

JE SUIS PARIS

JE SUIS LONDRES

B

The 9/11 attacks refer to a series of coordinated terrorist attacks that took place in the USA on 11 September 2001. They were carried out by the extremist Islamic terrorist group Al-Qaeda, and included flying two airplanes into the World Trade Center towers in New York City. Around 3,000 people died in the attacks, and thousands more were injured.

A   This photograph of a man falling from the North Tower of the World Trade Center during the 9/11 attacks is one of the most widely seen images from the mass tragedy.
B   The slogan 'Je suis Charlie' was used to show solidarity with the victims of the attacks on *Charlie Hebdo* magazine in 2015. It has also been used in reference to numerous terrorist attacks that followed.

The 9/11 attacks on the World Trade Center in New York City transformed the nature of international security. In the years since, the growing conflict and instability in the Middle East have had significant ramifications for Western democracies. The past few years have seen terrorist attacks linked to Islamic extremism in Belgium, France, Germany, Sweden, Britain and the USA. Increasingly, 'home-grown' terrorists have perpetrated these attacks.

The fear generated by these attacks has led governments in democracies around the world to introduce counter-terrorism measures that severely undermine individual rights.

In response to the 9/11 attacks, the Patriot Act was passed in the USA, which included provisions to enhance state surveillance, the authorization of indefinite detention of immigrants and permission for law enforcement officers to search homes and businesses without the occupant's knowledge. More generally, counter-terrorist measures have led to the extensive surveillance of the population by the government, and in some cases the use of torture. Trump even floated the idea of a 'Muslim registry' in the USA. Such a registry would represent a huge violation of human rights by discriminating against a group based on its religious beliefs. It is especially shocking because it echoes the registration of Jewish people in Nazi Germany, which was one of the first stages in the Nazi persecution of Jews.

As previously discussed, the growing concerns about security since 2001 have led to an increase in the popularity of far-right groups in Europe, who have sought to use public fear of terrorist attacks to justify the need for strong authoritarian leaders, to reject the human rights agenda and to link the refugee crisis resulting from the conflict in Syria to the rise of terrorism. In countries such as Britain, France and Germany, calls from these groups for immigration controls are rooted in anti-Islamic rhetoric. This is also evident in other countries around the world such as the USA, where Trump called for a 'Muslim ban', which would restrict entry to the USA from a number of Muslim-majority countries.

A

B

A   Anti-Muslim graffiti defaces a Shi'ite mosque at the Islamic Center of America in Dearborn, Michigan, in 2007. Trump used and fuelled prejudice against Muslims during his election campaign.
B   There has been a rise in stereotyping and prejudice towards Muslims in the USA and Europe since the 9/11 attacks, which populist leaders have used to bolster their support.
C   This campaign was launched to raise awareness about, and counter, growing Islamophobia. Far-right groups have used rising Islamophobia to call for more authoritarian leaders, greater immigration control and a rejection of human rights protection.

c

Big data refers to very large volumes of data that can be analyzed computationally (with modern data-processing software) to reveal patterns and trends that especially relate to human behaviour and interactions.

This climate of fear has allowed authoritarian leaders leaders, such as Orbán and Trump, to come to power on the basis that they will not allow democratic processes, such as rule of law and respect of individual rights, to prevent them from implementing tough measures that guarantee the security of the majority.

The sinister use of new technology provides a further challenge to democracy.

Initially, there was a great deal of optimism that widespread access to the Internet and social media sites would serve to strengthen democracy. Increased flow of information, greater opportunities for people to express their opinions and engage with fellow citizens, and potential for increased interactions between citizens and governments were all seen as ways that technology could improve how democratic systems function.

Instead, technology is being used to undermine democratic processes. From the unrestricted spread of populist messages and fake news stories to the use of big data to manipulate potential voters, there are growing concerns that social media is fuelling the tide of right-wing populism.

Cambridge Analytica, a technology company specializing in data analysis and strategic communication, worked with both the Trump election campaign and the Leave campaign in the Brexit referendum. The company collected masses of data about millions of voters from social media sites, such as Facebook, and claimed to have used this data to provide detailed psychological profiles to better understand people's emotions and beliefs. The company then claimed to have crafted individual messages to manipulate voters. For many, this represents a hijacking of democracy by one of the most effective propaganda machines ever seen.

Elections around the world have also increasingly faced the problem of computer hacking. Candidates' personal information and emails have been accessed by hackers who have released this information to the wider public with the deliberate objective of influencing the outcome of the elections. In the case of the hacking of Hillary Clinton's emails during the 2016 US presidential elections, there have been widespread accusations that the Russian government was involved. This has led to growing concerns that democratic processes are being derailed by foreign interference.

A

A   Street art from graffiti artist Banksy highlights the extreme levels of surveillance in Britain in 2008. Increased surveillance in democracies has increasingly been justified on the basis of counter-terrorism. However, such extensive surveillance can undermine people's democratic freedoms and basic rights. As well as infringing on citizens' privacy, it provides governments with greater unchecked power.
B   This piece by Banksy also highlights the prevalence of surveillance cameras in 2008. The British government passed a bill in 2016 giving intelligence services sweeping powers of surveillance, including tools for snooping and hacking. There was little public response. Such surveillance systems are particularly worrying in democracies with rising authoritarianism. They provide autocrats with the tools for political repression.

B

This is especially worrying because countries believed to be complicit in this cyber warfare, such as China and Russia, actively support the rise of this new authoritarianism.

There are investigations under way into the use of big data to manipulate voters and the hacking and release of political candidates' personal data. However, at the present time it is not clear that the current checks and balances in democratic systems can deal with this emerging threat. In the French elections in 2017, the electoral authorities warned the media and Internet users that they would be prosecuted if they published documents obtained from a hack attack on Emmanuel Macron's political campaign (because this would violate a law that puts a 24-hour ban on reporting during election day). This appears to have worked, as none of the illegally obtained documents were published. However, it is clear that this is an issue that needs a much bigger systematic response if elections are to remain free and fair in the future.

Emmanuel Macron (b. 1977) is the current president of France. He assumed office in 2017. Prior to this, he was the minister of economy, industry and digital affairs of France.

A

The World Values Survey is a global research project that since 1981 has conducted representative national surveys in close to 100 countries that look at people's values and beliefs, and how they change over time.

Perhaps the biggest challenge facing democracy today is widespread citizen indifference and disengagement.

An influential 2017 study of attitudes to democracy in North America, Western Europe, Australia and New Zealand, by Roberto Stefan Foa and Yascha Mounk, found that citizens in these established democracies have grown jaded and cynical about the value of democracy as a political system. Across all of the countries, people have become far less hopeful that they can do anything to influence public policy. The study, based on data from the World Values Survey, found that young people are especially dissatisfied with democracy: they are less supportive of free speech, more into political radicalism, less likely to object to military coups, and less inclined to see civil rights as absolutely essential. Compared with previous generations, young people also feel elections are less important.

This growing apathy is a worrying trend. For democracy to survive, it is essential that citizens believe in its value and engage with democratic processes.

What prevents leaders from abusing their power in democracies is the system of accountability, whereby citizens are aware of what leaders are doing and are willing to vote them out of office for violating the rules and procedures of democratic systems. As seen in India's Emergency, if people feel that democratic processes are becoming an obstacle to positive change, there is little to prevent leaders from gradually dismantling the institutions of democracy.

Some have suggested this falling support for democracy is because people have grown used to highly stable democracies, and consequently take democracy for granted. While this may in part be the case, it would be a mistake to assume that there is nothing more to declining engagement with democracy than this. Given the growing economic insecurity many people face, there are genuine grounds for discontent with the current global system.

The response to this should be to deepen democracy rather than abandon it.

B

A   A 'non-voting booth' in Manhattan, New York City, in 2014. The booth was part of an election-day intervention by the students of the School of Visual Arts Products of Design department to understand why young people do not vote, and to address the problem of voter apathy.
B   There is growing frustration with the current state of democracy. 'Error 404' signs are used at political protests to indicate this sense of disillusionment with democratic politics.

Conclusion

A

B

C

Democracy around the world has faced a number of significant challenges since the 2008 global financial crisis. But as discussed in previous chapters, democracy has encountered numerous difficulties since its emergence.

The topsy-turvy history of democracy would suggest that it is perhaps too soon to talk of democracy failing.

This does not, however, mean that the threat to democracy since 2008 is not a serious one, or that there is no urgent need to respond. There is.

A   Shepard Fairey designed the 'We the People' poster series to protest Trump's presidential inauguration. It features people from ethnic minorities in response to Trump's demonization of such groups.

B   The posters, including this one with a Muslim woman wearing a US flag hijab, emphasize the shared humanity and diversity of the USA, and seek to counter rising right-wing nationalism.

C   Taking its name from the first line of the US Constitution, the 'We the People' poster series challenges people to uphold the values espoused in the US Constitution.

D   Bihari people protest their mass eviction in Dhaka, Bangladesh, in 2017. These Urdu-speaking refugees, with homelands in modern-day India and Pakistan, have faced severe discrimination.

This response has already begun in many places. Since the US presidential elections in 2016, there has been a surge of peaceful protests to counter the creeping authoritarianism described in Chapter 4. The women's march against Donald Trump was the largest day of protests in US history, and these marches occurred all over the world. There have also been protests in countries such as Poland and India, calling for the protection of the rule of law and for the rights of minority groups. This civil society action is essential for countering the efforts to undermine democratic governance. As we have seen, citizen engagement is at the very heart of democracy.

There are signs that the surge in populist groups promoting illiberal politics has, to some extent, been checked in Europe. Elections since Trump became president have seen parties across the political spectrum hold off the threat from populist parties that seek to weaken democratic processes. However, it is important that this is not taken as a sign to return to 'business as usual' in democratic countries. There are various limitations of democracy that need to be addressed if we are to truly call democracy a success.

We need to shift our understanding of what democracy is.

The dominant view still seems to be that democracy is simply about the preferences and will of the majority in society. Elections and public preferences are, of course, fundamental to how democracy works. But there are other parts of the system that are equally important.

These include protecting the basic human rights of everyone in society. They also include the rule of law, supported by an independent judiciary and a free press. Another crucial part of the democratic system is ensuring that everyone in society has the opportunity to participate in politics and civil life, whatever their views. The threat to democracy discussed

A   *The Riot Club* (2014) is about a long-established elite drinking club at Oxford University, priding itself on hedonism, with powerful political connections. The film is widely believed to be based on the real-life Bullingdon Club.

B   ' Untitled' (1996) by Richard Billingham is from the series *Ray's a Laugh*, which captures the everyday lives of the artist's parents, Elizabeth and Ray. The photographs show the poverty the couple live in as a result of Ray's alcoholism.

A

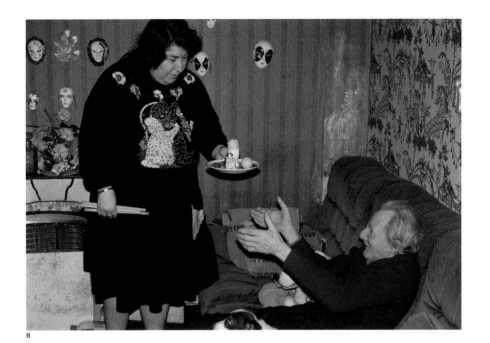

B

in this book is based on one part of the system – popular support – being used to undermine the other parts. Therefore, we need to move towards an under-standing of democracy that recognizes the importance of all the different pillars that support the democratic system.

There is an urgent need to tackle the huge inequalities of wealth, income and opportunity. These growing inequalities are a major reason for the threat that democracy is facing. If democracy is to survive, it must address the needs of everyone in society, especially those who are worst off. Therefore, improving the living standards of those on lower incomes is a priority. It is vital that democracy is not hijacked by the wealthiest in society, and that the constraints on government power are not used to prevent change that would bring benefits across different groups.

Democracy remains the best form of government to deliver this change. Consequently, it is essential that there is a deepening and strengthening of democratic processes if a rejection of democracy is to be avoided. The threat to democracy since the 2008 financial crisis demonstrates that democracy is built on shallow foundations in much of society. To strengthen the basis of democracy, there needs to be far greater effort to engage people in democratic politics. This will help ensure that democratic processes continue to improve.

Striving to enhance democratic processes is, itself, at the core of democracy. It is worth reflecting on the fact that when Alexis de Tocqueville wrote his hugely influential book on how democracy succeeded in the USA in the middle of the 19th century, some people were still enslaved by others and women had no political rights. In fact, in the USA, the abolition of slavery was 30 years away, the extension of suffrage to women was more than 50 years away, and the 1965 Voting Act, which guaranteed all Americans the right to vote, was more than 100 years away. These eventual changes were all the result of immense struggle.

Democracy is the most effective form of government because it provides people with the space and opportunity to address the problems they face as a society.

A

A MPs of the Palikot Movement wear masks to protest against the Polish government signing the Anti-Counterfeiting Trade Agreement in 2012, which many felt would increase Internet censorship. Guy Fawkes masks have become a symbol of political protest.

B Burqa-clad women cast votes in Kandahar in 2009. Polling stations opened for the second ever presidential elections in Afghanistan, held under tight security amid Taliban threats to disrupt voting.

C Fully veiled Iraqi women flash the sign for victory with their ink-stained fingers, showing they had voted in Iraq's first parliamentary election (2014) since US troops withdrew.

B

C

Throughout the history of democracy, people have come together to push for change in society, and this change has been achieved through the process of democracy. Consequently, democracy has delivered more in the way of individual freedom, sustained prosperity, peace and dignity. However, it is clear that there is still a long way to go. In the future, we are likely to continue to face security threats, economic difficulties and problems emerging from climate change.

A healthy democracy will be essential to meet these challenges.

Further Reading

Acemoğlu, Daron and Robinson, James A., *Why Nations Fail: The Origins of Power, Prosperity and Poverty* (London: Profile, 2012)

Arendt, Hannah, *The Origins of Totalitarianism* (New York: Penguin Books, 2017 [1951])

Bitar, Sergio, and Lowenthal, Abraham F., *Democratic Transitions: Conversations with World Leaders* (Baltimore: John Hopkins University Press, 2015)

Bose, Sumantra, *Transforming India: Challenges to the World's Largest Democracy* (Cambridge, MA: Harvard University Press, 2013)

Brennan, Jason, *Against Democracy* (Princeton, Princeton University Press, 2016)

Cheeseman, Nic, *Democracy in Africa: Successes, Failures and the Struggle for Political Reform* (Cambridge: Cambridge University Press, 2015)

Chomsky, Noam and Herman, Edward, S., *Manufacturing Consent: The Political Economy of the Mass Media* (New York: Pantheon, 1988)

Collier, Ruth Berins, *Paths toward Democracy: The Working Class and Elites in Western Europe and South America* (Cambridge: Cambridge University Press, 1999)

Dahl, Robert A., *Democracy and its Critics* (New Haven: Yale University Press, 1989)

De Tocqueville, Alexis *Democracy in America: and Two Essays on America* (London: Penguin Books, 2003 [1835])

Diamond, Larry, *The Spirit of Democracy: The Struggle to Build Free Societies Throughout the World* (New York: Holt and Co., 2008)

Fanon, Frantz, *The Wretched of the Earth* (London: Penguin Books, 2001 [1961])

Fukuyama, Francis, *The End of History and the Last Man* (London: Penguin Books, 1992)

Grayling, A.C., *Democracy and Its Crisis* (London: Oneworld, 2017)

Hay, Colin, *Why We Hate Politics* (Cambridge: Polity, 2007)

Hayek, Friedrich A., *The Road to Serfdom* (London: Routledge, 2001 [1944])

Haynes, Jeff, *Democracy in the Developing World: Africa, Asia, Latin America and the Middle East* (Cambridge: Polity, 2001)

Held, David, *Models of Democracy* (Cambridge: Polity, 1987)

Hunt, Lynn, *Inventing Human Rights: A History* (W. W. Norton & Co., 2007)

Huntington, Samuel P., *The Third Wave: Democratization in the Late Twentieth Century* (Norman: University of Oklahoma Press, 1991)

Jones, Owen, *The Establishment: And How They Get Away With It* (London: Penguin Books, 2014)

Mandela, Nelson R., *Long Walk to Freedom: The Autobiography of Nelson Mandela* (London: Bayback Books, 1994)

Mansbridge, Jane J., *Beyond Adversary Democracy* (Chicago: University of Chicago Press, 1980)

Milanovic, Branko, *The Haves and the Have-Nots: A Brief and Idiosyncratic History of Global Inequality* (New York: Basic Books, 2011)

Moore, Barrington, *The Social Origins of Dictatorship and Democracy: Lord and Peasant in the Making of the Modern World* (Boston: Beacon Press, 1966)

Mounk, Yascha, *The People vs. Democracy: Why Our Freedom is in Danger and How to Save It* (Cambridge: Harvard University Press, 2018)

North, Douglass C., Wallis, John Joseph and Weingast, Barry R., *Violence and Social Orders: A Conceptual Framework for Interpreting Recorded Human History* (Cambridge: Cambridge University Press, 2013)

Nussbaum, Martha C., *Not for Profit: Why Democracy Needs the Humanities* (Princeton, Princeton University Press, 2010)

Phillips, Anne, *Engendering Democracy* (Philadelphia: Pennsylvania University Press, 1991)

Plato, *The Republic* (New Haven: Yale University Press, 2006)

Przeworski, Adam, Alvarez, Michael E., Cheibub, José Antonio and Limongi, Fernando, *Democracy and Development: Political Institutions and Well-Being in the World, 1950-1990* (Cambridge: Cambridge University Press, 2000)

Putnam, Robert D., *Bowling Alone: The Collapse and Revival of American Community* (New York: Simon & Schuster, 2000)

Rice, Condoleezza, *Democracy: Stories from the Long Road to Freedom* (New York: Twelve, 2017)

Rodrik, Dani, *The Globalization Paradox: Why Global Markets, States and Democracy Can't Coexist* (Oxford: Oxford University Press, 2011)

Roy, Arundhati, *Field Notes on Democracy: Listening to Grasshoppers* (Chicago: Haymarket Books, 2009)

Schumpeter, Joseph A. *Capitalism, Socialism and Democracy* (Abingdon: Routledge, 2013 [1942])

Sharp, Gene, *From Dictatorship to Democracy: A Conceptual Framework for Liberation* (Boston: The Albert Einstein Institute, 1994)

Sen, Amartya, *Development as Freedom* (Oxford: Oxford University Press, 1999)

Skocpol, Theda, *Diminished Democracy: From Membership to Management in American Civic Life* (Norman: University of Oklahoma Press, 2003)

Tilly, Charles, *Democracy* (Cambridge: Cambridge University Press, 2007)

Varoufakis, Yanis, *And the Weak Suffer What They Must? Europe's Crisis and America's Economic Future* (London: The Bodley Head, 2016)

West, Cornel, *Democracy Matters: Winning the Fight Against Imperialism* (New York: Penguin Books, 2004)

Zakaria, Fareed, *The Future of Freedom: Illiberal Democracy at Home and Abroad* (New York: W. W. Norton & Co., 2003)

Picture Credits

Every effort has been made to locate and credit copyright holders of the material reproduced in this book. The author and publisher apologize for any omissions or errors, which can be corrected in future editions.

a = above, b = below,
c = centre, l = left, r = right

2 Tim Stubbings / Alamy Stock Photo
4–5 Liu Xingzhe / VCG via Getty Images
6–7 Photos 12 Archive / Diomedia
8 a Popperfoto / Getty Images
8 b Everett Collection Inc / Alamy Stock Photo
9 Bettmann / Getty Images
10 Jonas Gratzer / LightRocket via Getty Images
11 Liu Xingzhe / VCG via Getty Images
12 Library of Congress, Washington, D.C.
13 Library of Congress, Washington, D.C.
14 Otto Herschan / Getty Images
15 Paula Bronstein / Getty Images
16–17 Musée du Louvre, Paris
18 Beinecke Rare Book & Manuscript Library, Yale University
19 Musée d'Orsay, Paris
20 Beinecke Rare Book & Manuscript Library, Yale University
21 Courtesy Ahmed Kathrada Foundation. Photo Herb Shore

22 l Universal Images Group / Diomedia
22 r Aristotelis Sarrikostas
23 Palazzo Madama, Rome
24 Piers Howell / Alamy Stock Photo
25 l From *Oscar II En Lefvandsteckning*, Andreas Hasselgren, 1908, Stockholm
25 r Stockholm Stadtmuseet
26 British Library, London
27 British Library, London
28 Ian Dagnall / Alamy Stock Photo
29 l Private collection
29 r State Hermitage, St Petersburg
30 Musée Carnavalet, Paris
31 SuperStock RM / Diomedia
32 VintageCorner / Alamy Stock Photo
33 Classic Image / Alamy Stock Photo
34 Archive Pics / Alamy Stock Photo
35 Keystone / Hulton Archive / Getty Images
36 Private collection
37 Popperfoto / Getty Images
38 Pictorial Press Ltd / Alamy Stock Photo
39 a Keystone / Getty Images
39 bl, bc Pictorial Press Ltd / Alamy Stock Photo
39 br Everett Collection Historical / Alamy Stock Photo
40 NARA / Franklin D. Roosevelt Library (NLFDR), New York
41 Mark Kauffman / The LIFE Picture Collection / Getty Images

42 akg-images / GandhiServe e.K.
43 a Popperfoto / Getty Images
43 b Universal Images Group / Diomedia
44 Elliott Erwitt / Magnum
45 AFP / Getty Images
46 l Chris Niedenthal / The LIFE Images Collection / Getty Images
46 r Wojtek Laski / East News / Getty Images
47 Aizar Raldes / AFP / Getty Images
48 Denis Farrell / AP / Rex / Shutterstock
49 al Jonathan Rashad / Getty Images
49 ar Mosa'ab Elshamy / Getty Images
49 bl Mohammed Abed / AFP / Getty Images
49 br Claudia Wiens / Alamy Stock Photo
50–51 Charles Platiau / Reuters
54 l Heritage Image Partnership Ltd / Alamy Stock Photo
54 r Private collection
55 l Courtesy William F. and Harriet Fast Scott Soviet Military and Cold War Collection, University of Kentucky Libraries, Lexington
55 r Private collection
56 l, ar Shiv Kiran / Fseven Photographers
56 br STR / AFP / Getty Images
57 Alberto Tamargo / Getty Images
58 Banaras Khan / AFP / Getty Images
59 Geoff Wilkinson / Rex / Shutterstock

Index

References to illustrations are in **bold**.

Acknowledgments:
The author would like to thank Jacob F. Field,
David Hudson, Lucas Leemann, Slava J.
Mikhaylov, Nicola Chelotti, Lior Erez, Patricia
Hardwicke, Nick Watts, Tristan de Lancey, Jane
Laing, Becky Gee, Rose Blackett-Ord, Sunita
Gibson, Jo Walton and Phoebe Lindsley for their
invaluable advice and feedback on this book.

This book is dedicated to my mother, Aruna,
my brother, Tejus, and to the memory of my
father, Padam.

Is Democracy Failing? © 2018
Thames & Hudson Ltd, London

General Editor: Matthew Taylor
Text by Niheer Dasandi

For image copyright information, see pp 138–139

First published in 2018 in the United States of
America by Thames & Hudson Inc., 500 Fifth
Avenue, New York, New York 10110

Library of Congress Control Number: 2018932292

ISBN 978-0-500-29365-2

Printed and bound in Hong Kong through Asia
Pacific Offset Ltd